How to Succeed in This Course

to accompany

Gerow
Psychology: An Introduction
Fifth Edition

prepared by

Josh R. Gerow
Indiana University--Purdue University at Fort Wayne
and
Judi M. Misale
Truman State University

 LONGMAN

An Imprint of Addison Wesley Longman, Inc

New York • Reading, Massachusetts •Menlo Park, California • Harlow, England
Don Mills, Ontario • Sydney • Mexico City • Madrid • Amsterdam

How to Succeed in This Course
to accompany *PSYCHOLOGY: AN INTRODUCTION, FIFTH EDITION*
by Josh Gerow

Copyright © 1997 Addison-Wesley Educational Publishers Inc.

ISBN: 0-673-97908-3

97 98 99 00 01 9 8 7 6 5 4 3 2

HOW TO SUCCEED IN THIS COURSE is divided into two parts. For the first, entitled *Effective Study*, textbook author Dr. Josh Gerow advises you on how to maximize your understanding of psychology through a practical, focused system of study. The second part, prepared by Dr. Judi M. Misale of Truman State University, consists of *Chapter Learning Objectives and Outlines*.

These tools are designed not only to assist you as you work through this particular course, but also to teach you the effective learning habits essential for successful performance at the collegiate level.

EFFECTIVE STUDY

EFFECTIVE STUDY

Psychologists study many things, most of which are practical and relevant to our everyday lives. Among the issues that psychologists have investigated are the factors that influence efficient and effective studying behaviors. It is appropriate to introduce some of the advice that comes from this research now, as we get started. I firmly believe that if you put this advice into practice, your performance in this course will benefit directly. We'll return later to many of the points raised here—mostly in our discussion of learning and memory. As we go along, I'll point out how some of the features of this book can make your study of psychology easier.

CONTENTS

HOW TO IMPROVE YOUR LEARNING AND MEMORY

How people learn things, and how they might learn and remember more effectively, are concerns that predate psychology. They are concerns that can be traced to ancient times. What has always surprised me is that after all these hundreds of years, the list of factors known to have a direct and significant impact on learning and memory is really quite short. Throughout this introduction, please keep in mind that effective study habits are not developed for their own sake, but in order to make learning more efficient. You don't go to college to study; you go to college to learn.

Set Goals and Motivate Yourself to Reach Them We are all aware that we can learn some things "by accident," without intending to do so. Our most efficient learning, however, takes place when we intend to learn, when we make a conscious, concerted effort to acquire new information. In a way, this is saying that it helps to be motivated to learn. And we can motivate ourselves to learn. One thing that helps is to establish goals.

Difficulties in learning often arise when college students do not have clear goals. Some may not have the foggiest notion of why they are in college in the first place, and thus can find no particular reason for doing well in their classwork. So it is a good idea to clarify in your own mind just why you are in college, why you are taking an introductory course in psychology, and why it is important to you (not to someone else) to do well in the course.

Make the Material You Are Learning Meaningful If you have never studied French, you would certainly find it easier to learn a list of 12 English words than to memorize a list of 12 French words. The reasons are clear: You know what the English words mean; they make you think of other words; you can associate them with other things; you know how they are used. The French words strike you as nonsense; you can't relate to them in a meaningful way.

This example can be generalized to other areas. The learning of any new information will be easier to the extent that that information can be made personal, meaningful, and useful. To a large degree, this means fitting the new information in with your past experiences and your plans for the future. To help you with this task, I've included many examples of the psychological concepts introduced in the text. The catch is that my examples are particularly meaningful to me. This may help you, but it would be much more useful for you to generate your own examples.

1

Practice, Practice, and Practice Some More   In Chapter 6 we will *define* learning to be the result of practice. Practice or rehearsal is an integral part of learning. Learning—academic learning in particular—is not something that happens automatically. Acquiring new information involves working with the material, studying it, practicing it. The more you practice any material, the better it will be retained. I'll have more to say about the quality of practice shortly, but for now: *With regard to practice, more is better than less.*

How you distribute practice time is extremely important. The research on this point is clear: Efficiency is improved when study time is interrupted with rest breaks. For most students and most courses, the recommended schedule is 45 minutes of study followed by a 15-minute rest break. So take short breaks. Get up and stretch, take a stroll, get a drink of water, and so on. But be careful—15 minutes of study followed by 45-minute breaks isn't going to be very efficient.

To encourage spaced or distributed study is one reason why I have divided each chapter into **Topics** and have inserted several **Before You Go On** sections within each Topic. They provide cues as to where a good place might be to take a break. To sit down and study a whole chapter straight through, without a break, is tough, and not a very efficient use of your time. Please notice that simply dividing a chapter into two, or three, or even four Topics doesn't make that chapter any longer or more difficult—in fact, dividing it into Topics will make it easier.

Get Feedback on Your Learning   A person with little or no knowledge of how his or her learning is progressing will be at a distinct disadvantage compared to a person who is informed. The process involved is what psychologists call "knowledge of results," or feedback. Imagine learning how to shoot basketball free throws while blindfolded. With no information about how you are doing or where the ball is going, there's little reason to suspect that you'll ever get to be very good. The same argument holds true for any kind of learning.

Some of the feedback that you get in college comes when your instructor evaluates your work. Use returned exams and papers as feedback. Review them, noting any errors you have made. Decide how your study habits can be changed to minimize errors in the future.

You can also provide yourself with important—and less costly—feedback by testing yourself on the material you are studying. Self-testing should be an ongoing process, but it is particularly useful as exams approach. For this course, you have three readily available means of providing yourself with feedback or knowledge of results: the **Before You Go On** questions within chapters, the **Test Yourself** questions at the end of each chapter, and the **Student Study Guide** that comes with the text.

Reward Your Effective Learning Behaviors   One of the most practical principles in psychology is that one's actions are often shaped by their consequences. Simply put, behaviors that are rewarded (later we will say *reinforced*) tend to get repeated whenever possible.

We all know the satisfaction that comes when our goals are met. That exhilarating feeling of doing well on a quiz, term paper, or lab report will go a long way to insure success in the future. As a college student, many of your rewards will probably come from instructors, friends, or family members. But you can't always depend on rewards from others to maintain your studying. Try to develop the habit of providing rewards for yourself for work well done. Study hard for 45 minutes, then reward yourself for putting in the honest effort (and by so doing, distribute your study time). Do something that will make you feel good. You'll be surprised at how something so simple can have such a significant impact on your behavior.

Think Critically About What Your Are Learning   To be of any use, the learning that occurs in a college course should involve more than just the memorization of facts. It should enhance one's ability to think critically about the subject matter. This is particularly true of a psychology course.

Many of us have a tendency to accept without question what we are told by people we perceive to be experts. I am now challenging you to do otherwise. To be sure, I believe that the information I have included in this text is as accurate and honestly presented as such information can be. But do not accept what is said here (or any place else) without thinking—critically—about that information. To think critically doesn't mean just to be negative. More than anything else, it means to question, in your own mind, from your own point of view, in the context of your own experience, what is being presented. Thinking critically about what is presented here is an important way to make the information meaningful, and we know that that helps learning.

What sorts of questions should you ask about the ideas presented in your psychology class? There are many, but here are a few suggestions: Where did this information or conclusion come from? On what sort of research was it based? Are there any data at all to support what is being claimed? Are there any other ways in which these results can be explained? Does this information fit my own personal experience? How might this conclusion be biased? Given this information, what other possibilities come to mind?

In order to stimulate your thinking about the material in this text, there is a section at the end of each chapter called **Thinking Critically About. . . .** As the name suggests, these questions do not have one "best" answer. They simply raise issues worth thinking about and points to ponder.

Work to Improve Your Performance   Let's make an important distinction. Learning is a process that takes place *inside* an individual. We cannot see it as it occurs. We cannot measure it directly. We can only infer learning from performance. You may think that your little nephew can play a tune on the piano—indeed, he has told you that he has learned to do so. If you really needed to know if he had learned that tune, what would you do? You'd ask him to demonstrate what he has learned. You would ask him to perform. The same sort of situation exists in the college classroom.

Put simply, learning involves acquiring new information, while performance involves retrieving that information when it is needed. And justifiably or not, it is your performance—based on what you've learned—that is evaluated. Your performance, not your learning, earns your grades in the classroom, or your raise or promotion in the workplace. So to do well in a college class is a two-phase process. First you must learn the required material and then you must be able to retrieve it from memory when it is needed. In the next few pages, I'll elaborate on these general principles of learning by giving specific advice on how to get more out of class, how to use your textbook more effectively, and how to prepare for exams.

TIME MANAGEMENT FOR TODAY'S COLLEGE STUDENT

Here's a reality that causes problems for many of us: There are only 168 hours in each week. For many students, academic success is often a direct reflection of the extent to which these 168 hours are managed.

"Nontraditional" students were once thought of as students who were older, employed outside the home at least on a part-time basis, and living at home with household and family responsibilities. On many college campuses today, including my own, this description fits the majority of students. It is for this busy student, with many commitments outside the classroom, that time management is most critical.

A standard rule of thumb is the advice that one should spend three hours of study each week for every hour spent in class. Introductory psychology courses usually meet for about three hours a week, which means that the average student should begin a semester planning to *spend nine hours a week studying psychology*—in addition to going to class! Most of my students laugh when I tell them about this rule of thumb, but they also recognize that if they did study that much, they would have no trouble doing well in my class.

If you want to succeed as a college student, you have to schedule time (and a place) for studying as surely as you schedule time for sleep, meals, your job, taking out the trash, or driving the kids to their soccer games. In the process, don't forget what I've already said about distributing study time in small chunks rather than in large blocks.

One area of time management over which you have significant control is the number of classes in which you enroll each term. Here's what I tell my academic advisees: "Take your time. Enroll only in the number of classes you honestly feel that you can handle. Some day you will graduate, and no one—potential employer or graduate school committee, for example—is going to ask you how long it took for you to graduate. What they probably will ask you is how well you did—they'll ask about your grades. It seems to me much more reasonable to take 6 or 7 years to graduate with As and Bs than to rush through in 4 years with Cs."

GETTING THE MOST FROM THE CLASSROOM

"But I never missed a class!" is the claim instructors often hear from students who have not done well on an exam and who have not learned the difference between attending a class and taking an active part in class. The difference has a significant impact on how well students learn.

Prepare for Class   It is always easier to listen to and understand information you are familiar with than it is to listen to and try to understand totally unfamiliar information. To be sure, few lectures and class activities are designed to be about something you knew before you took the class. The material will have to be somewhat new; that is what you are paying for. But if you prepare and plan carefully, lectures and class discussions will not seem totally alien.

Once the term is under way, preparing for class will be relatively easy. You will have had time to "feel out" your instructor and develop a sense of what will be happening in class. At the very least you should have reviewed recent lecture notes and previewed the text for each meeting. Perhaps the most important thing to do is to familiarize yourself with the vocabulary that might come up in class. If you're familiar with vocabulary terms *before* you get to class, your listening for ideas and concepts will be easier because you will not have to think about new words. You will then have a chance to concentrate, to organize what is being said, and to summarize your thoughts in coherent notes.

Most good listening is a matter of attitude. To be an effective listener, you must be in the proper frame of mind. As you take your seat, you have to rid your mind of thoughts of the trivial activities of the day. You cannot do a good job of listening to a lecture if you are thinking about last night's date or this afternoon's lunch. You can't contribute to a discussion if all you want to talk about is last weekend's game. You must be thinking about psychology. Get your mind warmed up: What's the instructor going to talk about today? What contributions will you be expected to make? How will today's class fit in with what you've already learned? How can you relate this material to your own personal experience? When you find yourself totally surprised at what is being said in class, you have not prepared correctly.

Develop Your Listening Skills Listening is an active process in which you relate what is being said to what you already have stored in your memory. It is a matter of taking in new information and organizing and storing it in such a way that it can be used again at some later time. Given the large amounts of information headed toward you in the classroom, active listening will require considerable concentration on your part.

We don't often think of it as such, but listening is a skill—one that can be developed just like bicycle riding, typing, or reading. Proficiency in listening can be increased through practice. Listening in class for new and useful information is different from listening to casual conversation or your favorite radio station. This is because a larger portion of the information will involve new or technical vocabulary, and because you will be expected to recall the information at some later time (on exams). Every time you listen in class you are practicing a basic learning skill.

In this regard, let me share with you my advice on the use of tape recorders in the classroom. I don't prohibit them in my classes, but I advise against their use. I'd rather have students force their attention and concentrate the first time around. Knowing that there's a "backup tape" can lead some students to take a lazy attitude toward listening in the first place.

Take Useful Notes Class attendance and careful listening are important because lectures are presented to you only once. Therefore, you will need some written record of the information presented orally in class to study and review later. Good lecture notes written in your own words are as valuable as a summarized and organized compilation of classroom instruction.

There is a large body of research devoted to note-taking skills. For now, we will consider just two basic principles you can use—principles that will help you learn psychology or any other discipline.

Principle 1: Select and Organize the Material Presented to You. It will soon become apparent to you, if it isn't already, that there is no way that you can write down everything your instructor says in class. This can be an advantage. Note-taking should be an active process of selecting and organizing the information you write down. Although it generally is better to take too many notes than it is to take too few, you must be an active listener who participates in class—not just a mechanical writer.

The notes you take will be *your* notes, so put them in a form you can use. Except for technical terms and new vocabulary, use your own words. In this way, your notes will be more meaningful to you when you review them. Copying information is not learning it.

You should develop some shortcuts—alternatives to writing everything out in longhand. The key here is flexibility. Feel free to abbreviate, but only if you will be able to understand your own symbols and notes when you go back to study later. Illegible or incoherent notes are worse than useless: You have wasted valuable listening time writing them.

There will be times when it is best not to take any notes at all. Participating in a class discussion or asking questions may be most beneficial. Once again, one of the best ways to learn new material is to get involved, to work *with it and make it personal.Principle 2: Edit and Review Your Notes.* Once class is over, only part of your work is done. During the class period you have been listening, selecting, organizing, participating, thinking, and writing. Now you should go back over your written record of the class. This is best accomplished in three stages.

1. Immediately after class, while the material is still fresh in your mind, review your notes, fill in gaps, underline for emphasis, note unclear sections that will require further work, and use the margins in your notebook to add information you simply did not have time to record.
2. Several times a week, as part of your study for each course, continue the editing process. Use your textbook, other notes, outside readings, or consult with your instructor for correct spellings, missing details, and the like.
3. An important stage in reviewing your notes should occur after each examination in a course. Go back and critically evaluate your own notes. To what extent did they help? How can they be improved? Did you write too much? Too little? Was the **format the best one possible?**

GETTING THE MOST FROM YOUR TEXTBOOK

For any class you take, you will find that there is more information stored in your textbook than could ever be presented in class. Since this is the case, learning how to get information from your text is one of the most important skills you can acquire in college. This is not to devalue the role of your instructor or class attendance. Instructors update text material, interject personal experience and points of view, and emphasize what they believe to be the most important sections of assigned readings. Here are a few general ideas to guide your study.

Prepare for Textbook Study Because textbook study is so important, you should develop expectations about the material in each chapter by reading the chapter preview, skimming the summary, and glancing at the headings, subtitles, and illustrations. Before you actually begin reading/studying the text, you should have a series of questions in mind. If nothing else, you should begin each chapter by asking questions such as: "What in the world is *this* all about?" "How can this be of any use to me?" "How can I relate any of this to what I already know?" "Where is this material going to show up on our next classroom exam?" In order to help you frame such questions, we begin each chapter in this text with a complete, detailed **Chapter Outline** and a chapter **Preview**.

Don't Read Your Textbook the Way You Read Other Books Perhaps the most significant insight about textbook study is that it is very different from casual reading. Reading a chapter is not studying a chapter. Studying is a process in which you must become actively and personally involved. Studying a text requires a great deal more concentration and mental effort than does reading for pleasure. What is the author trying to say? What are the major ideas? What evidence supports those ideas? What are the minor points? How can the material be related to what you already know from personal experience, previous reading, or classroom lectures? How will this information show up on a test?

There are times when you should look up from the book, pause, and think about what you have just read. You should be able to quickly summarize the material in your own words, which is why **Before You Go On** questions are included within each chapter of this book. If you cannot answer these questions, there is little point in going further. Go back over the section you've just read. Speed may be fine, but speed without comprehension is a waste of time.

Effective textbook study is a skill that can be learned by anyone, but it will not be learned automatically. It takes hard work and practice to develop textbook study skills. The rewards for your work, however, will be almost immediate.

Make Textbook Study an Active Process There is no doubt that you must be mentally active and alert while studying so you can search, question, and think. This text and its accompanying Study Guide have been designed to facilitate active studying. *If you have not done so yet, please go back now and read the section of the Preface titled "Features of this Text."*

Underlining or highlighting in textbooks has become a common practice. Unfortunately, it often is misused. The purpose of underlining is to emphasize particular passages of the text so essential points can be reviewed by simply restudying underlined passages. The mistake that many students make is to underline too much: When 80 percent of a page is underlined for emphasis, the remaining 20 percent usually appears more striking.

You can increase the value of your textbook for studying by using the margins of the text for your personal notations. Make your text a storehouse of references. Cross-reference textbook material with information in your notes. If it's your book, use it—write in it.

PREPARING FOR EXAMS

Few occasions are quite as pleasant as the one you experience when you walk into class to take a big exam, fully prepared, confident that you know the material and that you are going to do well. I also know from personal experience just how miserable it feels to face an exam unprepared, doomed before you begin, unable to understand—much less answer—the first question. The key lies in being prepared. Proper preparation for exams helps to furnish the kind of positive reinforcement that education is meant to provide, but it isn't easy. You'll have to schedule your time, test your progress, and engage in continuous, active review.

Rule 1: Prepare on a Daily Basis -- Don't Cram   This rule is a simple restatement of a point I made earlier about the value of spaced or distributed practice.

In almost every case, you will be notified of upcoming tests or examinations well in advance. Often, scheduled exams are noted on the course outlines handed out on the first day of class. Most of your exams should come as no surprise to you. The secret to good exam performance is that daily preparation is needed.

To be truthful, preparing daily isn't an easy task. It's difficult to sit down today to study for an exam that's three weeks away. With so much time before the exam, it seems that there will be plenty of opportunity for studying later.

On the other hand, daily preparation is not all that special. It involves the sort of things I mentioned above. Preparing for and carefully listening in class is daily preparation, as are taking good notes and editing and reviewing them soon after class. A crucial step in preparing for exams is to make a complete, realistic schedule. If you study your textbook on a regular basis, you won't even have to consider cramming for exams.

Rule 2: Find Ways to Test Yourself   As examination day approaches, you will want some indication of just how well your studying has been progressing. To be most effective, this self-testing should begin well in advance of any examination date. There are many techniques for evaluating your own achievement, all of which involve constructing, taking, and "grading" your own test on assigned material before your instructor does. For example, if you think that you may have to identify the important structures of the eye, try to draw a picture of one, labeling all of the structures you can think of, and then check your drawing with the one in your book. If you know that your next exam will ask for the definitions of new terms and concepts, see how many you can write out on your own.

Again, you should find two features of this text helpful: the **Before You Go On** questions, which follow every major section of every chapter, and the **Test Yourself** sections, which are found at the end of each chapter.

I am convinced that self-testing is the best thing you can do to prepare for classroom exams. Perhaps I'm soft-hearted, but I tend to believe those students who come to me after a test and say—with teary eyes and quivering lips—''But I read the book, over and over. I know the material.'' They probably did read the book over and over. They probably did learn a lot of psychology in the process, and that is certainly a good thing. But classroom tests do not measure what you have learned. They measure what you can remember. Students often spend too much time putting information into memory, and too little time getting information out of memory, which is what is being tested.

Imagine that you have just finished studying the section on the history of psychology in Chapter 1 of this book. I'd like to think that that material is presented clearly and in a form that is easy to understand. Let's say you agree. Having read this section, you can honestly say to yourself, "I understand all that. I appreciate some of psychology's history. I learned something." Now comes the crucial part in which you have to ask yourself, "How is this going to show up on the classroom exam?" You've got at least three things you can do: (1) You can check the **Test Yourself** sections at the end of each chapter; (2) you can check the **Student Study Guide** to see how it tests the material you've just read; or (3) you can pretend that you are the instructor and make up your own practice items. This last option actively involves you in the process of exam preparation, even though it takes time to develop the skill of writing test items.

Rule 3: Strengthen Learning with Review If you have maintained a schedule of daily preparation and have consistently evaluated your own performance, you should be able to approach examination day with confidence. There is no way that everything you'll need to know for an exam can be assimilated the night before. You simply cannot understand and digest large amounts of material hours before an exam. However, it is well worth your time to review the material that is to be on the exam. To review means "to look at again." You should certainly review just before an exam. A more helpful procedure is to review on a regular basis throughout the term. You should be constantly reviewing what you've learned. Research evidence and common sense tell us that most forgetting occurs soon after learning. Frequent review, however, can improve retention significantly.

A Final Word on Exam-Taking When you take an exam, you are being asked to perform on the basis of what you have learned. Although the effects of anxiety on learning are subtle, the effects of anxiety on performance are well known. Your performance will be poor if you become overly anxious, upset, and uptight—even if you have learned the material reasonably well. Just realizing that anxiety may reduce your efficiency does little to help. Anxiety is very difficult to eliminate by sheer force of willpower. The most effective way to reduce anxiety is to deal with its cause. If you have conscientiously applied yourself to the job of preparing for an exam, you should have reduced—if not eliminated—the most common cause of test anxiety. If being overly nervous about taking exams becomes a source of concern for you, consider talking to someone in the counseling center, learning lab, or psychology department who can help you with this problem. (We'll discuss related issues in Chapter 11 when we bring up strategies for dealing with stress.)

WHAT ABOUT THE SQ3R METHOD?

In this last section, I want to take the ideas we have been talking about and recast them in a slightly different way. Nearly half a century ago a teacher named Francis Robinson described a strategy for studying that he called the SQ3R Method. The method is highly recommended for two reasons: (1) It is simple; (2) it works. Although you are sure to recognize that there is nothing new here, thinking about your studying in this way may be helpful. SQ3R can be rewritten S-Q-R1-R2-R3. All we have to do is to see what these letters stand for.

S = Survey. The idea here is to anticipate what you are about to study by looking ahead, reading the chapter outline, the chapter Preview, skimming the Summary, and quickly glancing through the chapter. You should try to get an overview of what is going to come up during your reading and studying.

Q = Question. As you might have guessed, this is the one point of the five in the list that I feel is most important. The idea is to continually ask yourself questions about what you are reading. If nothing else, stop from time to time and ask what I call *The Universal Study Question:* "Whaaa?"—in the sense of: "What did I just read about?" As it happens, you get considerable help in this book because we're going to keep asking you questions in the **Before You Go On** sections.

R1 = Read. Once you've surveyed and questioned, the time has come to get to it and read the text. Remember: Don't try to sit down and read the entire chapter from beginning to end. Go for smaller sections and space or distribute your practice.

R2 = Recite. We usually think of reciting in terms of performing out loud, as in a "recital." In this instance, you needn't be so literal. The basic idea is to "talk to yourself" about what you're reading. Having surveyed the chapter, you've formed some questions and are now reading the chapter. By "recite" we mean that the time has come to answer those questions. Really. Go ahead and try to answer the **Before You Go On** questions, for example. Yes, in this book answers to **Before You Go On** questions are provided in the **Summary**. But don't just turn back there and read MY answer. Try to provide an answer on your own first.

R3 = Review. See, we *have* been through all this, haven't we? By review, Robinson meant what we meant when we talked about reviewing earlier. You should plan to schedule time to go back over your notes and the text, testing yourself anew each time. Just because you "knew" the answer to a question yesterday doesn't mean that you know it today. To find out: review.

CHAPTER LEARNING OBJECTIVES

and

CHAPTER OUTLINES

CHAPTER 1

WHAT PSYCHOLOGISTS DO

TOPIC 1A – What is Psychology?

Learning Objectives  ✓ *Done*

1. Describe why we may claim that psychology is a science.

2. Explain why psychologists are sometimes referred to as scientist-practitioners.

3. Describe the subject matter of psychology and the use of operational definitions.

4. Describe psychology's roots in philosophy and science.

5. Discuss how Descartes, Locke, Darwin, Fechner and von Helmholtz influenced psychology.

6. Compare and contrast structuralism and functionalism.

7. Discuss the contribution of women to the early development of psychology.

8. Describe behaviorism and how it differs from structuralism and functionalism.

9. Discuss psychoanalysis as an approach to psychology.

10. Describe the two approaches that have challenged behaviorism: humanism and Gestalt psychology.

11. Discuss the contributions to early research on the brain-behavior connection by such researchers as Gall, Flourens, Fritsch and Hitzig, and Berger.

12. Describe five general themes and principles that appear repeatedly throughout the study of psychology.

I.   The Goals of Psychology: Science and Practice

    A.   Psychology is the scientific study of behavior and mental processes.
    B.   One goal of psychology is to use scientific methods to discover and understand relationships that exist among these behaviors and mental processes.
        1.   A science is composed of an organized body of knowledge.
        2.   Psychology's body of knowledge has been gained through scientific methods.
    C.   A second goal of many psychologists is to apply the results of scientific investigation to real-world situations.

II.   The Subject Matter of Psychology

    A.   The subject matter of psychology consists of behavior and mental processes: external and internal events.
        1.   Behavior is what organisms do and is observable and potentially measurable.
        2.   Psychologists study two types of mental processes: cognitions and affects.
    B.   Psychologists use operational definitions to define their subject matter.
        1.   Operational definitions define concepts in terms of the procedures used to measure the concepts.
        2.   Because they specify how a behavior is measured, operational definitions help us communicate accurately with others.

III.   Psychological Approaches Past and Present

    A.   No two psychologists approach their subject matter in exactly the same way, because they differ in the individual experiences, expertise, values, and prejudices they bring to their study.
    B.   The formal roots of psychology can be found in both philosophy and science.
        1.   The philosophers suggested it is reasonable to seek explanations of human behaviors at a human level.
        2.   Charles Darwin, Gustav Fechner, and Hermann von Helmholtz contributed to the progression of science during the nineteenth century.
    C.   Wilhelm Wundt founded the first psychological laboratory at the University of Leipzig in 1879.
    D.   William James believed that the mind could not be broken into parts and structures but that the adaptive functions of the mind should be the focus of study, a philosophy called functionalism.
    E.   Women such as Mary Floy Washburn, the first woman awarded a Ph.D. in psychology, Mary Calkins, and Christine Ladd-Franklin contributed to the early formation of psychological science.
    F.   Behaviorism is an approach to psychology emphasizing the overt, observable, measurable behavior of organisms, and is most associated with John Watson and B. F. Skinner.
    G.   Psychoanalytic psychology, an approach that emphasizes the influence of the unconscious and instincts on behavior and thought, traces its roots to Sigmund Freud
    H.   Humanistic psychology, whose leaders were Carl Rogers and Abraham Maslow, is an approach emphasizing the person or self as a central matter of concern.
    I.   Gestalt psychology, which was begun in the early 1900s by a group of German scientists (most notably Max Wertheimer) focused on how we select and organize information from the outside world.
    J.   Early researchers such as Franz Joseph Gall, Pierre Flourens, and Hans Berger studied the relationship between structures of the brain and the behavior of organisms.
    K.   There are over 500,000 psychologists in the world today, with about half of these working in the United States.

IV.   Key Principles in Psychology

    A.   Behaviors and mental processes result from an interaction of inherited, genetic influences and environmental influences.
    B.   Environmental diversity and experience plus the diversity of genetic material makes each individual unique.
    C.   Psychology is relevant to our daily lives because it has practical applications in the real world.

TOPIC 1B – The Research Methods of Psychology

Learning Objectives   Done

1. Define naturalistic observation, and discuss the potential problems with its use.

2. Explain how surveys and case histories are used in psychology.

3. Discuss advantages and disadvantages of surveys and case histories.

4. Explain the function of a correlation, and discuss when this method is appropriate.

5. Describe the data needed to calculate a correlation coefficient.

6. Explain the meaning of positive, negative, and zero correlation coefficients.

7. Understand the process of doing an experiment, and be able to identify and define independent, dependent, and extraneous variables.

8. Name and explain the major benefit provided by experimental research that is lacking in observational and correlational research.

9. Explain how matching, random assignment, and baseline designs contribute to control in experiments.

10. Explain the general process of meta-analysis and its contribution to research.

11. Discuss the ethical considerations that are unique to psychological research for both human and animal participants.

One

I.   Observational Methods

   A. Naturalistic observation involves carefully and systematically watching behaviors as they naturally occur.
   B. Surveys, which ask a sample of respondents the same question or set of questions, are a means of collecting observations from a large number of subjects by interview or questionnaire, and they yield data difficult to get otherwise.
   C. A case history provides in-depth information on one or a few persons studied over a long period of time because it examines a wide range of variables using various techniques, such as interviews or psychological tests, to gather data.

II. Correlational Methods

   A. Correlation is a statistical procedure that can be used to assess the nature and degree to which sets of observations are lawfully related.
       1. A correlation coefficient may range from -1.00 to +1.00.
       2. The sign in front of the correlation coefficient indicates the direction of the relationship, i.e., whether it is positive or negative.
       3. The absolute value of the correlation coefficient indicates the strength of the relationship.
   B. Cause-effect conclusions are inappropriate for correlational studies, even when two responses are highly correlated.

III. Experimental Methods

   A. Experimental methods involve a set of operations that investigates relationships between manipulated (independent variables) and measured events (dependent variables), both of which must be operationally defined.
   B. To have confidence in the results of an experiment, control must be exercised in the experimental situation, particularly control of extraneous variables.
   C. Meta-analyses is a statistical technique that has become very popular.

IV. Ethics In Psychological Research

   A. Ethical considerations are essential to the gathering of information.
   B. Ethical Principles of Psychologists is published by the American Psychological Association for practitioners and researchers.
   C. Human subject risk must be assessed in research, and animal guidelines are also stringent.

CHAPTER 2

THE NERVOUS SYSTEMS AND BEHAVIOR

TOPIC 2A – Nerve Cells and How They Communicate

Learning Objectives

 Done

1. Describe the main structural features of a neuron.

2. Explain the function of each structure.

3. Describe myelin, and explain the functions it serves in the central nervous system.

4. Discuss the basic process involved when a neuron fires, describing the involvement of resting and action potentials.

5. Explain the concept of neural threshold and the all-or-none effect.

6. Explain how neural impulses are transmitted at the synapse.

7. Name four neurotransmitters, and indicate a psychological process in which each is involved.

8. Explain the relationship between nicotine and acetylcholine.

9. Name the divisions of the human nervous system, and indicate how they relate to one another.

10. Describe the function of the endocrine system.

11. Name three glands in the endocrine system, and describe their functions.

I. The Neuron

    A. Neurons are individual nerve cells, the basic units of the nervous system; there are approximately 100 billion neurons in the human brain.

    B. Most neurons have certain structures in common.
        1. The cell body is the largest mass of the cell and contains the genetic information.
        2. Dendrites extend out from the cell body and receive messages from other neurons.
        3. Along the axon, which extends away from the cell body, neural messages travel toward other neurons.
        4. Myelin is a white, fatty covering or sheath for axons that serves to protect the neuron and speed impulses.

    C. No neurons are generated (or replaced) after birth, which makes them unique among cells.

    D. The function of a neuron is to transmit neural impulses from one place in the nervous system to another via electrical and chemical means.
        1. Neurons are filled with and surrounded by fluids containing chemical particles called ions, which have a positive or a negative charge.
        2. The resting potential is the electrical charge of a neuron at rest, about -70 mV.
        3. The charge of the neuron changes when it is stimulated to fire; the new charge, the action potential, is about +40 mV.
        4. The all-or-none principle refers to the fact that when a neuron is stimulated, it either transmits an impulse or it does not.
        5. The minimal level of stimulation required to get a neuron to fire is call the neural threshold.
        6. The intensity of a stimulus relates to the number of neurons involved and the rate at which they fire.

II. From One Cell to Another: The Synapse

    A. The synapse is the general location where an impulse is relayed from one neuron to another.

    B. Axon terminals relay information from one neuron to the dendrites or soma of neighboring neurons.
        1. Axon terminals contain small pockets called vesicles.
        2. Vesicles contain complex chemicals called neurotransmitters.

    C. Neurotransmitters are released into the synaptic cleft, the space between the axon terminals of one cell and the membrane of the next cell, that can either excite or inhibit the neighboring cell.

    D. About 60 neurotransmitters are known, some are more researched than others.
        1. Acetylcholine (ACh) is implicated in normal memory function, as well as memory problems such as those accompanying Alzheimer's disease, and it commonly works in synapses between neuron and muscle cells.
        2. Norepinephrine appears to be involved in mood regulation, and is related to feelings of arousal and anxiety.
        3. Dopamine also seems to be involved in mood regulation and with the impairment of movement.
        4. Endorphins are natural pain suppressors.

III. Human Nervous Systems: The Big Picture

    A. The central nervous system (CNS) includes the neurons in the brain and the spinal cord.

    B. The peripheral nervous system (PNS) is composed of all other neurons and is divided into two parts.
        1. The somatic nervous system serves the skeletal muscles and picks up impulses from the major sensory receptors.
        2. The autonomic nervous system is divided into two parts that activate the smooth muscles and glands and provide feedback to the CNS about internal processes: the sympathetic division is activated during emotional excitement, and the parasympathetic division is active during relaxation.

    C. The endocrine system is a network of glands (including the pituitary, thyroid, and adrenal glands) that secretes hormones into the bloodstream and interacts with the nervous system to affect behavior.
        1. The pituitary gland is often called the "master gland" because of its direct control over many other glands in the system, e.g., thyroid, adrenal and sex glands.
        2. The thyroid gland produces a hormone called thyroxin that regulates the rate at which oxygen is used and the rate of body function and growth.
        3. Adrenal glands are located on the kidneys, and they secrete a variety of hormones into the bloodstream.

TOPIC 2B – The Central Nervous System

Learning Objectives *Done*

1. Describe the major features of a spinal reflex.

2. Explain why spinal cord injury sometimes causes paralysis.

3. Discuss the two brain stem structures, their location, and their functions.

4. Describe the cerebellum, its location, and its major function.

5. List the location and major functions of the RAS, limbic system, hypothalamus, and thalamus.

6. Discuss the role the basal ganglia plays in Parkinson's disease.

7. Describe the location and function of the four lobes of the cerebral cortex.

8. Identify the primary sensory, motor, and association areas of the cerebrum.

9. Explain the split-brain procedure.

10. Describe how split-brain operations facilitate the study of brain functions.

11. Briefly summarize the respective functions of the right and left hemispheres.

12. Discuss whether there are any significant differences between the brains of females and males.

Outline – Topic 2B

I.   The Spinal Cord *Done*

    A.   The spinal cord is a massive collection of interconnected neurons–including sensory, motor and interneurons–within the spinal column that is protected by the hard bone and cartilage of the vertebrae.
    B.   The spinal cord rapidly transmits neural impulses to and from the brain, and plays an important role in spinal reflexes.

II. The "Lower" Brain Centers

    A.   Lower brain centers, parts of the brain other than the cerebral cortex, are physically located below the cerebral cortex and were first to develop in an evolutionary and a developmental sense.
    B.   Lower brain structures are most clearly shared with other animals.
    C.   The brain stem, which includes the medulla and the pons, is just above the spinal cord.
    D.   The cerebellum smoothes and coordinates body movements; damage disrupts fine, coordinated movement.
    E.   The reticular activating system is a network of nerve fibers that begins in the brain stem and goes to the top of the brain.
    F.   The limbic system is a collection of small structures that controls many instinctive, complex behaviors, that is involved in displays of emotion, and that is involved in the formation memories. (hippo)
    G.   The hypothalamus mediates motivational and emotional behaviors.
    H.   The basal ganglia is a collection of structures that produces and depends on dopamine to control large, slow body movements.
    I.   The thalamus acts as a relay station between the cerebral cortex and lower brain structures.

III. The Cerebral Cortex

    A.   The cerebral cortex is the large, convoluted outer covering of the brain that is the seat of cognitive functioning and voluntary action.
    B.   The cortex is divided into left and right cerebral hemispheres.
    C.   Each hemisphere is divided into four lobes: the frontal lobe, the temporal lobe, the occipital lobe, and the parietal lobe.
    D.   The cerebral cortex can be divided into three major areas and mapped for different functions: the sensory areas located at the front of the parietal lobe receive information from the sense receptors; the motor area, a strip at the back of the frontal lobes, is where conscious, voluntary control of muscle activity originates; and three association areas. (not occipital)
    E.   The two cerebral hemispheres have different functions.
       1.   The left hemisphere, the larger hemisphere in most humans, is believed to be dominant and is responsible for the production of speech and the use of language, as well as the processing of analytical information.
       2.   The right hemisphere is credited with expression and interpretation of emotions, along with the processing of visual information.
    F.   Research shows few differences between male and female brains other than those directly related to reproductive function.

CHAPTER 3

SENSATION AND PERCEPTION

TOPIC 3A – Sensory Processes

Learning Objectives

1. Define sensation.

2. Define perception, and discuss the factors that may affect the process.

3. Define psychophysics, and explain the notion of absolute and difference thresholds.

4. Discuss ways the concepts of absolute and difference thresholds may be useful in the real world.

5. Discuss the basic ideas of signal detection theory, and explain how the theory might provide a clearer picture of sensory sensitivity.

6. Explain the concept of sensory adaptation, and discuss how dark adaptation differs from normal sensory adaptation.

7. Explain the physical characteristics of wave amplitude, wavelength, and wave purity, and discuss how these physical properties of light waves affect our psychological experience of light.

8. Discuss the major eye structures and their functions.

9. Understand the physical characteristics of the fovea and the blind spot.

10. Discuss rods and cones: the visual processes attributed to each and the differences between the two.

11. Summarize the trichromatic and opponent-process theories of color vision, and understand empirical support for each theory.

12. Explain the physical characteristics of sound: wave amplitude, wave frequency, and wave purity, and discuss how these physical properties affect our psychological experience of sound.

13. Explain the path of sound waves through the different structures of the ear.

14. List the primary qualities of taste, and discuss the current knowledge about their locations.

15. Describe the cutaneous senses and list their transducers.

16. Explain the position senses and how they operate.

17. Explain the type of stimulation that can produce the sensation of pain.

18. Discuss theories explaining how pain is processed in the brain.

19. Describe methods by which the sensation of pain can be controlled or reduced.

I.   Preview

   A.   Sensation is the process of receiving information from the environment and changing that input into nervous system activity.
   B.   Perception is concerned with the selection, organization, and interpretation of stimuli.

II. Sensory Thresholds

   A.   Psychophysics is the study of the relationship between the physical attributes of stimuli and the psychological experiences they produce.
   B.   Absolute thresholds, although hard to determine in reality, for purposes of study are defined as the physical intensity of a stimulus that a subject reports detecting 50 percent of the time.
   C.   Difference thresholds are the minimal difference between stimulus attributes that can be detected.
   D.   Signal detection theory proposes that stimulus detection involves a decision-making process of separating a signal from background noise (both sensory and environmental).
   E.   Sensory adaptation is a process in which sensory experience tends to decrease with the continued exposure of a stimulus; dark adaptation, on the other hand, refers to the eye's ability to become *more* sensitive to light after a prolonged time in the dark.

III. Vision

   A.   Light is radiant energy that can be represented in wave forms called light waves.
   B.   Light waves have three major physical characteristics, each with its own psychological correlate: wave amplitude (brightness), wavelength (hue), and wave purity (saturation).
   C.   Vision involves changing light-wave energy into neural energy.
   D.   Most structures in the eye, however, serve not to transduce energy, but to focus visual images.
       1.   Light enters the eye through the cornea, the transparent outer shell of the eye, and next travels through the pupil, an opening in the pigmented, or colored, portion of the eye, the iris.
       2.   Ciliary muscles focus the visual image by changing the shape of the lens.
       3.   The aqueous humor is the liquid between the cornea and lens that nourishes the cornea and the structures at the front of the eye; the vitreous humor is a liquid behind the lens whose major function is to keep the eyeball rounded.
   E.   It is at the retina that light energy is changed to neural energy.
       1.   Photoreceptors (rods and cones) at the very back of the retina transduce light waves into neural energy.
       2.   The two main features of the retina are the fovea and the blind spot.
   F.   Rods and cones differ distinctively in number, in location, and in function.
   G.   Visual information continues to be altered along a path to the visual area of the occipital lobe.
   H.   Theories of color vision try to explain how the eye codes different wavelengths of light to produce different experiences of color.
       1.   The trichromatic theory proposes that the eye contains three distinct receptors for color, each receptor responding best to one of three primary colors.
       2.   The opponent-process theory proposes three *pairs* of visual mechanisms that are sensitive to either blue or yellow, red or green, and black or white.

IV. Audition (Hearing)

   A.   The stimulus for hearing is sound.
   B.   Sound is principally a series of pressures of air that beat against our eardrums.
   C.   Like light waves, sound waves have three major physical characteristics, each with a psychological correlate: amplitude (loudness), frequency (pitch), and purity (timbre).
   D.   Deep inside the ear sound waves are changed into neural impulses, and as with the eye, most ear structures simply transfer energy from without to within.
       1.   The pinna collects incoming sound waves and funnels them inward, where they beat against the eardrum causing vibrations that are transmitted to the ossicles in the middle ear.
       2.   The main organ of the inner ear is the cochlea, which contains the actual receptor cells for hearing.

V. The Chemical Senses

    A. Taste (gustation) is stimulated by chemical molecules that are dissolved in liquid, and smell (olfaction) is stimulated by chemical molecules that are dissolved in air.

    B. The experience of taste and smell are highly interrelated.

    C. Taste (gustation) has four basic psychological qualities–sweet, salty, sour, and bitter–and the receptor cells for taste are located in the tongue.

    D. Smell (olfaction) originates in receptor cells located high in the nasal cavity, very close to the brain.

VI. The Skin, or Cutaneous, Senses

    A. Each square inch of our skin contains nearly 20 million cells, including a large number of sense receptors.

    B. Warm and cold temperatures appear to be registered at different locations on the skin.

        1. However, specific receptor cells for hot or cold have not been located.

        2. In fact, the experience of hot appears to result from the simultaneous stimulation of both warm and cold spots.

VII. The Position Senses

    A. Position senses allow us to know how and where our bodies are positioned in space with respect to gravity.

    B. There are two systems of position sense over and above what vision can provide.

        1. The vestibular sense provides information about balance, gravity, acceleration, or deceleration via receptors located in five fluid-filled chambers (three semicircular canals and two vestibular sacs) near the inner ear on both sides of the head.

        2. Our kinesthetic sense provides information about the movement or position of our muscles and joints.

VIII. Pain: A Special Sense

    A. Pain can signal that problems are occurring somewhere in our bodies, but it is a private sensation and is often difficult to share or describe.

    B. Very intense stimulation of virtually any sense receptor can produce pain, but so can small amounts of stimulation (e.g., a pinprick).

    C. Pain receptors are found both on the skin and within the body.

    D. Pain is experienced in our brains, and while it is believed the thalamus is involved, no specific center for pain has been identified in the cerebral cortex.

    E. The gate-control theory of how pain is experienced proposes a gate-like mechanism high in the spinal cord that signals for the gate to be opened or closed so that pain messages do, or do not, get to the brain.

    F. A cognitive-behavioral theory of pain also stresses central mechanisms, noting the influence of attitudes, cognitions, and behaviors on the experience of pain.

    G. Techniques can be used to minimize, or manage, the experience of pain.

        1. Drugs can inhibit pain messages at the level of the spinal cord and at the specific pain site.

        2. Hypnosis and cognitive self control can effectively lessen feelings of pain.

        3. Placebo effects demonstrate that psychological processes can inhibit pain.

        4. Counterirritation, or forceful stimulation near the location of pain, can lessen the experience of pain.

        5. Acupuncture can be an effective treatment of pain, although scientists don't know yet why it works.

    H. Individual responses to pain are unique and are influenced by many factors.

        1. Prior experience, memory, feelings about pain; one's cognitions, affect, behavior; or gender and cultural factors may affect pain responses.

        2. In Japan, individuals are socialized not to show pain, and in Western cultures, men are often similarly socialized.

        3. Such factors may create problems in the diagnosis or treatment of conditions where pain is an informative symptom.

TOPIC 3B – Perceiving the World Around Us

1. Explain the process of perception.

2. Discuss the effect of stimulus factors on perceptual selectivity.

3. List and explain the personal factors that impact attention.

4. Define the Gestalt concept of figure-ground relationship.

5. Discuss the basic Gestalt principles of perceptual organization.

6. List and define the ocular and physical cues that provide us with information about depth and distance.

7. Define the following perceptual constancies: size, shape, brightness, and color.

8. Discuss the known characteristics of, and knowledge about, illusions.

I. Paying Attention: A Process of Selection

 A. Stimulus factors, characteristics of stimuli that make them more notable than others, influence our selection of stimuli from the environment, primarily through contrast effects.
  1. The more intense a stimulus, the more likely we are to notice it, although context can affect the percept; e.g., intense noise in a very noise environment may not get our attention.
  2. Objects that differ in size from others within the same context are more noteworthy.
  3. Motion is a powerful factor in determining visual attention.
  4. Repetition influences selection, provided we have not adapted to the stimuli.
  5. Brightness, color, or loudness are also ways in which stimuli may differ.
 B. Personal factors, such as motivation, expectation, and past experiences, sometimes influence what gets attended to.
 C. Although perception of stimuli usually occurs without conscious effort, several factors influence the process.
  1. We are doing bottom-up processing when we attend to a stimulus because of its particular characteristics and later organize, identify, and store that stimulus in our memory.
  2. Top-down processing occurs when stimuli are perceived in a certain way because of concepts or information already processed by the perceiver.

II. Organizing Our Perceptual World

 A. Perceptual organization involves organizing the bits and pieces of information that are received by our senses into meaningful, organized wholes.
 B. Gestalt psychologists studied ways that we group together and organize stimuli to form meaningful gestalts, or patterns.
  1. Gestalt is a German word meaning whole, configuration, or totality.
  2. Figure-ground relationship is the Gestalt principle that stimuli are selected and perceived as figures against a background.
  3. The manner in which stimuli are grouped and organized, which is also affected by many factors, intrigued Gestalt psychologists.
 C. Bottom-up processing refers to forming gestalts–organizing into meaningful units–by putting stimuli together based on their characteristics, or stimulus factors.
  1. Proximity (or contiguity) is the Gestalt principle of organization by which stimuli are perceived as belonging together if they occur close together in space or time.
  2. Similarity states that stimulus events that have similar properties (e.g., color) tend to be grouped together perceptually.
  3. Continuity is the principle of organization by which a segment of stimulus is perceived as continuing in the same direction in which it began.
  4. Common fate, an organizational principle that applies to moving stimuli, describes our tendency to group together elements of a scene that appear to move in the same direction and at the same speed.
  5. Closure, one of the most commonly encountered principles of organization, refers to our tendency to perceive incomplete figures as whole and complete; that is, we fill in the gaps.
 D. Motivation, expectation, and past experiences are personal factors that influence perceptual organization using top-down processing.
 E. We perceive our world three-dimensionally, even though light reflected from stimuli falls on our two-dimensional retina; not only do we know *what* a stimulus is, but we know *where* it is with considerable accuracy.
  1. Ocular cues–including physical cues, binocular, and monocular cues–are processes of the perceptual system that provide information about stimuli.
  2. Physical cues for depth and distance include linear perspective, interposition, relative size, texture gradient, patterns of shading and light, and motion parallax.
  3. Even something as rudimentary as depth and distance perception appears to by culturally influenced.
 F. Because of perceptual constancies, such as size constancy, shape constancy, brightness constancy, and color constancy, we recognize familiar objects as being the same regardless of fluctuations on the retina.
 G. Geometric illusions and impossible figures are experiences in which our perceptions are at odds with what we know as physical reality.

CHAPTER 4

VARIETIES OF CONSCIOUSNESS

TOPIC 4A – Consciousness: Awake and Asleep

Learning Objectives ✓

1. Define consciousness.

2. Describe the notion William James had about normal waking consciousness.

3. Name and define the three levels of consciousness proposed by Freud.

4. Explain contemporary research regarding levels of consciousness.

5. Characterize unconscious processing, and provide an example of evidence for its existence.

6. Distinguish between the EEG and EMG.

7. Describe the four stages of sleep.

8. Explain how REM sleep differs from NREM sleep.

9. Describe the physiological changes that accompany REM sleep.

10. Discuss current hypotheses about why dreaming occurs.

11. Name and describe three common disorders of sleep.

I. Preview
   A. Wilhelm Wundt and William James actually defined psychology as the science of consciousness or mental activity.
   B. Consciousness refers to our awareness or the environment and of our own mental processes.

II. Normal Waking Consciousness

   A. According to William James, normal, waking consciousness has four characteristics: it is always changing, and it is personal, continuous, and selective.
   B. Studying human consciousness scientifically, or experimentally, has been a challenge to psychologists for some time.

III. Levels of Consciousness

   A. We seem to experience different levels of consciousness.
   B. The higher the level of consciousness, the better we are able to process information.
   C. Freud wrote that only a small portion of one's mental life was readily available to one's awareness at any given time, but empirically demonstrating the levels of consciousness proposed by Freud has been difficult.
   D. Current research indicates that we sometimes do process things without awareness, but there is lack of consensus about the dividing line between conscious and unconscious processes; present data indicate our unconscious level of awareness is simple, primitive, and unsophisticated in terms of the amount of information it can handle.

IV. Sleep and Dreaming

   A. Sleep is a normal process that alters consciousness by gradually reducing our alertness, awareness, and perception of events around us, yet it is not well understood.
   B. Stages of sleep can be measured by an electroencephalogram (EEG), which records the brain's electrical activity, or by an electromyogram (EMG), which records muscle activity, tone, or state of relaxation.
      1. In a relaxed, presleep stage, the brain produces alpha wave activity.
      2. Stage 1, which lasts about ten minutes, is light sleep characterized by theta waves.
      3. Stage 2 sleep is similar to stage 1 with the addition of sleep spindles.
      4. Stage 3 is getting into deep sleep characterized by twenty to fifty percent delta waves.
      5. Stage 4 is deep sleep dominated by delta waves, and represents about fifteen percent of a night's sleep.
   C. Sleep is divided between REM (rapid eye movement), during which dreams occur, and NREM (no rapid eye movement) stages.
      1. Dreams usually occurs about 90 to 120 minutes each night, roughly twenty to twenty-five percent of adult sleep.
      2. Atonia, which is a muscular immobility caused by the total relaxation of the muscles, occurs during REM sleep.
      3. Nevertheless, the REM sleeper may experience excitement of the sex organs, shallow and rapid breathing, and increased blood pressure and heart rates.
   D. On average, most people get about 1.5 hours less sleep each night than they need, and some get even less; "sleep debt" refers to the fact that sleep loss accumulates from one night to the next.
   E. Insomnia is the inability to fall asleep and/or stay asleep when one wants to.
      1. Nearly 30 million Americans have chronic, debilitating insomnia–women more commonly than men, and the elderly about one and a half times more often than younger adults.
      2. Pseudoinsomnia refers to the fact that people are actually sleeping, but believe they are not.
      3. Over-the-counter medications designed to treat insomnia may cause more harm than good.
   F. Narcolepsy is a disorder that involves unintentional sleeping and immediate REM sleep, sometimes accompanied by atonia, making it potentially quite dangerous.
   G. Sleep apnea involves patterns of sleep during which breathing stops entirely; if episodes are longer than a minute or two) potential consequences include hypertension, coronary heart disease, stroke, impotence, and memory loss.

TOPIC 4B – Voluntary Alternations of Consciousness

1. Define hypnosis and describe who can be hypnotized.

2. Describe meditation, and explain its proposed benefits.

3. Explain dependence, tolerance, withdrawal, addiction, and drug abuse.

4. List the effects of depressant drugs, and explain how such drugs work to elicit these effects.

5. Discuss the differences between the various different types of stimulant drugs.

6. Describe the effects of hallucinogenic drugs.

7. Explain how marijuana differs from the other drugs discussed.

I. Hypnosis

    A. Hypnosis is a voluntarily altered state of consciousness characterized by a marked increase in suggestibility, focused attention, exaggerated use of imagination, inability or unwillingness to act independently, and acceptance of reality distortion.

    B. Not everyone can be hypnotized; susceptibility to hypnosis varies considerably from person to person.

    C. The ability to engage easily in daydreaming and fantasy, as well as suggestibility and willingness, is correlated with hypnotizability.

    D. It's unlikely people will do things when hypnotized that they wouldn't do otherwise.

    E. Some believe hypnosis is no more that a heightened level of suggestibility, but others believe it to be a special state.

    F. Perceived pain can be reduced via hypnosis by using negative hallucinations.

    G. Hypnotized subjects are aware, at some level, of what is going on.

    H. Memory is probably not improved with hypnosis, nor is one's ability to learn new material.

II. Meditation

    A. Meditation is a self-induced state of altered consciousness characterized by a focusing of attention and relaxation.

    B. Meditation is generally associated with Eastern religions, but became popular in North America in the 1960s, at which time psychologists began to study the practice.

    C. One of the most popular types of meditation is Transcendental Meditation (TM).

    D. There are measurable physiological changes that occur during meditation.

    E. Doubts do exist about claims of benefits from meditation because researchers report no physiological differences, or differences in ability to cope with stress, pressure, or threatening situations, between meditating persons and people simply resting.

III. Altering Consciousness with Drugs

    A. Chemicals that alter consciousness by inducing changes in perception, mood, or behavior are referred to as psychoactive drugs.

        1. Dependence, which may be either physical or psychological, occurs when use of the drug is required to maintain functions.

        2. Tolerance refers to a condition where more and more of the drug is needed to produce the same effect.

        3. Withdrawal is a negative reaction that occurs when one stops taking the drug.

        4. Addiction refers to extreme dependency, with tolerance and withdrawal usually present.

        5. Drug abuse, contrasted with drug use, is characterized by a lack of control, a disruption of interpersonal relationships and/or difficulties at work, and maladaptive use that lasts at least one month.

    B. Stimulants–including caffeine, nicotine, cocaine, and amphetamines–activate the nervous system, producing a heightened sense of arousal coupled with mood elevation.

    C. Depressants reduce one's awareness of external stimuli, slow normal body functions, and decrease overt behavior; alcohol, opiates, heroin, and barbiturates are depressants.

    D. Hallucinogens have the most unpredictable effects on consciousness, the most common being visual hallucinations: LSD is the most popular and potent hallucinogen in most Western cultures.

    E. Marijuana is a mind-altering drug, but it does not fit into any of the previous three categories; in small doses it acts like a depressant, in higher doses it may act like a hallucinogen.

CHAPTER 5

LEARNING

TOPIC 5A – Classical Conditioning

Learning Objectives

1. Define learning and conditioning.

2. Summarize the essential process of classical conditioning.

3. Define acquisition, extinction, spontaneous recovery, generalization, and discrimination.

4. Describe the sorts of responses that are most readily influenced by classical conditioning.

5. Describe the "Little Albert" experimental demonstration.

6. Define phobic disorders and describe how systematic desensitization is used to treat such disorders.

7. Understand what makes an effective CS.

8. Discuss what taste aversion studies tell us about the relationship between the CS and the UCS.

Outline – Topic 5A

I.   What Is Learning?

   A. Learning is demonstrated by a relatively permanent change in behavior that occurs as a result of practice or experience.
   B. The most basic, fundamental types of learning are called conditioning.

II. Pavlov and a Classic Demonstration

   A. Ivan Pavlov, a Russian physiologist, received the 1904 Nobel Prize for his study of digestion.
   B. Pavlov's observation that the dogs would salivate at the sight of food–or the sight of the lab assistant–led him to study classical conditioning.
       1. Classical conditioning is a type of learning in which an originally neutral stimulus comes to evoke a new response after being paired with another stimulus that reflexively evokes that same response.
       2. The orienting reflex is the unlearned response of attention toward a new or unusual stimulus.
       3. Habituation is a simple form of learning in which an organism comes to ignore a stimulus of no consequence.
   C. The classical conditioning paradigm consists of the presentation of the CS and the UCS, which then elicits the UCR–which later becomes the CR, though the CR seldom reaches the strength of the UCR regardless of the number of pairings.

III. Classical Conditioning Phenomena

   A. Acquisition is the stage of classical conditioning during which the strength of the CR increases.
   B. Extinction, the weakening and eventual cessation of the strength of the CS, occurs after a series of trials in which the CS is presented without the UCS.
   C. After rest, the CR may reappear upon presentation of the CS, which is called spontaneous recovery.
   D. Generalization occurs when a CR is elicited by stimuli that are different from, but similar to, the CS.
   E. Discrimination, the opposite of generalization, occurs when the organism is taught to respond only to one specific CS.

IV. The Significance of Classical Conditioning for People

   A. Classical conditioning has special significance because of its role in the acquisition of emotional responses to stimuli in the environment.
   B. Watson and Rayner's experiments with Little Albert are examples of conditioned fear.
       1. Albert was conditioned to be fearful of a white rat by pairing its presentation with a loud, unexpected noise.
       2. Watson and Rayner demonstrated that Albert's fear generalized to other stimuli.
       3. These experiments raised the issue of unethical treatment of human subjects.
   C. A phobic disorder is an intense, irrational fear that leads a person to avoid the feared object, activity or situation; phobias seldom extinguish on their own.
   D. Systematic desensitization was introduced by Joseph Wolpe, and consists of three stages: first, the therapist trains the client to relax; next, an "anxiety hierarchy" is constructed; lastly, each item in the hierarchy of anxiety-producing stimuli is paired with a state of relaxation.
   E. Systematic desensitization goes beyond extinction to a process known as counterconditioning, in which a new response is acquired to "replace" the former fear.

V.   Rethinking What Happens in Classical Conditioning

   A. Today conditioning is seen as an active search for sensible ways to represent the environment, a search for information that one stimulus gives about another.
   B. Blocking is a phenomenon where a second stimulus (paired with a CS and the UCS) remains a neutral stimulus and does not come to elicit a CR.
   C. The time interval between the CS and UCS can sometimes be on the order of hours.

TOPIC 5B – Operant Conditioning

1. Explain the principles of operant conditioning.

2. Discuss shaping, acquisition, extinction, and spontaneous recovery in operant conditioning.

3. Understand the operational definition of reinforcer.

4. Distinguish between positive and negative reinforcers.

5. Distinguish between primary and secondary reinforcers.

6. Explain intermittent schedules of reinforcement and the advantages of using each of them.

7. Discuss the notion of cognitive maps.

8. Explain the concept of latent learning.

9. Summarize the basic concepts of social learning theory.

10. Distinguish between "reinforcement" and "vicarious reinforcement."

I. The Basics of Operant Conditioning

    A. B. F. Skinner used the term "operant" to refer to a behavior that operates on the environment; operants are controlled by their consequences, and operant conditioning changes the probability or rate of responses on the basis of the consequences that result from those responses.
    B. Thorndike observed that responses are learned when they are followed by a satisfying state of affairs (Law of Effect).
    C. Skinner developed a special apparatus for demonstrating operant conditioning; he called it an operant chamber, but many psychologists refer to it as a "Skinner box."
    D. Operant conditioning involves several procedures.
        1. Shaping involves reinforcing successive approximations of the response.
        2. Acquisition is the stage of conditioning in which the response rate that follows reinforcement becomes more and more rapid.
        3. Extinction occurs when reinforcement is withheld and the response rate returns to baseline.
        4. Spontaneous recovery is the return of an extinguished response following a rest period.

II. Reinforcement

    A. Reinforcement is a process that increases the rate or probability of the response it follows.
    B. A positive reinforcer is a stimulus that increases (or maintains above baseline) the rate of a response that precedes it; a negative reinforcer is a stimulus that increases the rate of a response that precedes its removal.
    C. Primary reinforcers, usually biological or physiological in nature, are those that do not require any previous experience to be effective; secondary reinforcers acquire their reinforcing properties by being paired with primary reinforcers or because of prior learning experiences.
    D. A continuous reinforcement schedule (CRF) consists of reinforcing every response; with intermittent reinforcement schedules, such as fixed ratio, fixed interval, variable ratio, and variable interval, a behavior is reinforced less frequently than every time it occurs.

III. Punishment

    A. Punishment occurs when a stimulus decreases the rate or probability of occurrence of the response that preceded it; positive punishment refers to delivering, or adding, a painful, unpleasant stimulus following an inappropriate response, and negative punishment means removing, or subtracting, a pleasant, valued stimulus following an inappropriate response.
    B. In order for punishment to be effective it should be delivered immediately and consistently, and alternative behaviors should be introduced.

IV. Generalization and Discrimination

    A. Generalization occurs when reinforced responses that have been conditioned to a specific stimulus appear in response to other, similar stimuli.
    B. Discrimination learning means that responses made to appropriate stimuli will be reinforced, while responses made to inappropriate stimuli will be ignored or extinguished.
    C. Generalization and discrimination in operant learning are processes that apply across various populations in a variety of situations.

V. Cognitive Approaches to Learning

    A. Cognitive approaches to learning emphasize changes that occur within an organism's set of cognitions.
    B. Edward Tolman proposed the concept of latent learning, and used the term cognitive map to refer to the mental picture, or representation, of the learning situation or physical environment.
    C. The central idea of Albert Bandura's approach to learning (known as social learning theory) is that learning often takes place through observation of models.
        1. Observational learning is primarily concerned with the organization of response elements into new patterns of behavior at a symbolic level.
        2. Vicarious reinforcement or vicarious punishment refer to learning about the consequences of one's own behavior by simply observing what happens to someone else.

CHAPTER 6

MEMORY

TOPIC 6A – How Can We Describe Human Memory?

Learning Objectives

1. Define memory.

2. Discuss sensory memory, including its capacity and duration.

3. Describe how material is put into short-term memory and how long it is stored there.

4. Describe the capacity of short-term memory and how chunking affects this characteristic.

5. Discuss the nature of coding in short-term memory.

6. Discuss the issue of permanence in long-term memory.

7. Explain the controversy surrounding "repressed" memories.

8. Describe the problems with eyewitness testimony, and have a general understanding of what we do know through research on eyewitness memory.

9. Contrast elaborative rehearsal with maintenance rehearsal as a means of encoding information into long-term memory.

10. Name and describe three possible types of long-term memory.

11. Contrast early and later theories about how and where memories are formed.

12. Distinguish between retrograde and anterograde amnesia.

I.   Memory as Information Processing

    A. Memory is the capacity to encode, store, and retrieve information.
    B. Using memory is a complex series of cognitive processes that involves three interrelated steps, or stages.
        1. Encoding involves putting information into memory.
        2. Storage involves keeping it in memory.
        3. Retrieval involves getting information back out of memory.
    C. Some theorists support the concept of multistore models of memory, while other theorists favor a levels-of-processing model of memory.

II.   Sensory Memory

    A. The basic idea of sensory memory is that information from our senses is held briefly in sensory memory before being passed on to the sensory systems.
    B. Sensory memory involves the storage of large amounts of sensory information for very short periods of time.
    C. Sensory memory is viewed as a rather mechanical, or physical, type of storage because information is not encoded there, and information stored in sensory memory cannot be acted upon.

III. Short-term Memory (STM)

    A. STM, also known as working memory, is a separate level in human memory that has a limited capacity and, without the benefit of rehearsal, a brief duration.
    B. Research on the duration of STM processing can be traced to the Brown and Peterson experiments, reported independently in the late 1950s.
        1. Correct recall depends on the length of the retention interval.
        2. STM can be extended by maintenance rehearsal, which amounts to the simple, rote repetition of information already in STM.
        3. As a general rule of thumb, the duration of STM is about fifteen to twenty seconds.
    C. George Miller described the capacity of STM as being five to nine (seven, plus or minus two) bits of information, although "chunking" information increases the capacity of STM.
    D. Conrad (1965) argued that information is represented acoustically in STM, meaning material is processed in terms of how it sounds, and subsequent research supports this view.

IV.   Long-term Memory (LTM)

    A. LTM refers to holding large amounts of information for long periods of time.
    B. There seems to be no practical limit to how much information can be encoded or processed into LTM.
    C. Many psychologists believe that information is permanently stored and that forgetting is a failure of retrieval, but according to Loftus and Loftus (1980), the bulk of evidence for this permanent storage/failure of retrieval view is neither experimental nor reliable.
    D. Recently, considerable attention has been focused on the accuracy of LTM, particularly "memories" of childhood trauma and abuse.
    E. Another area where the accuracy of LTM has been called into question is eyewitness testimony, where research shows reports by eyewitnesses may sometimes be questionable.
    F. Encoding in LTM may result from rote repetition (maintenance rehearsal) or elaborative rehearsal in which the information is reorganized and made meaningful.
    G. Information in LTM may be processed by different types of LTM, including procedural memory, semantic memory, and episodic memory; these types are distinct, but they interact.

V.   Where and How are Memories Formed in the Brain?

    A. Karl Lashley attempted to discover the particular parts of the brain that are responsible for memory, but concluded that memories do not reside in specific locations in the brain.
    B. Later research suggests certain types of memories may be found at particular locations, e.g., sensory memories.
    C. It is still not clear how memories are formed, but recent research suggests alteration of the nervous system at the level of the neuron or synapse.

TOPIC 6B – Improving Memory: Factors Affecting Retrieval

Learning Objectives

1. Describe how measures of recall, recognition, and relearning assess the ability to retrieve.

2. Define implicit tests of retention.

3. Describe how the context in which information is encoded affects the ability to retrieve that information.

4. Define meaningfulness, and explain how it relates to retrieval.

5. Explain mnemonic devices and cite examples.

6. Define schemas, and explain how they affect retrieval.

7. Explain overlearning, massed practice, and distributed practice, and describe their effects on the ability to retrieve.

8. Distinguish between retroactive and proactive interference.

I.   How We Measure Retrieval

    A. Retrieval can be measured by direct, explicit methods.
        1. Recall, either free recall or serial recall, is a difficult retrieval task providing the fewest number of cues.
        2. Recognition, which is superior to retrieval by recall in virtually all cases, requires the subject to simply identify material learned previously.
    B. Indirect, or implicit, tests of memory demonstrate that information is stored in memory when previous experiences are taken advantage of without a conscious attempt to do so.

II. How We Encode Information

    A. Retrieval of information will be difficult if it was not encoded appropriately.
    B. Retrieval tends to be best when the context in which it takes place matches the context that was present at encoding.
    C. State-dependent memory means that to some degree, retrieval depends on the extent to which a person's state of mind at retrieval matches the person's state of mind at encoding.
    D. Strategies that encode information meaningfully help us to easily retrieve this information from LTM.
    E. Mnemonic devices are strategies for improving retrieval that are elaborative and that take advantage of existing information in memory.
        1. Organizing materials into a meaningful story is known as narrative chaining.
        2. Forming meaningful mental images at encoding aids remembering.
        3. The key word method of study involves visually tying two words together.
        4. The method of loci consists of visualizing a series of familiar locations and placing each item to be remembered at one location.
    F. A schema is an organized, general knowledge structure that is stored in long-term memory.

III. How We Schedule Practice

    A. Retrieval is a function of the amount of practice and how that practice is distributed.
    B. Practicing, or rehearsing, material over and above what is needed to just learn it is the process of overlearning.
    C. Retrieval can be improved if practice (encoding) is spread out over time with rest intervals in between.
        1. Massed practice (no breaks), in general, produces the poorest performance.
        2. An exception may occur if things are grouped or continuous (e.g., a complex math problem); in such a case things should be worked through to the conclusion.

IV. How We Overcome Interference

    A. A basic problem with retrieval may be interference.
    B. Retroactive interference involves interference from learning that occurs after the critical material is learned.
    C. Proactive interference occurs when previously learned material interferes with the retrieval of material learned later.
    D. Interference is less likely with meaningful, well-organized material.
    E. Interference increases as the interfering material becomes more similar to the material being retrieved.

CHAPTER 7

TOPIC 7A – INTELLIGENCE

Learning Objectives

1. Provide a theoretical and operational definition of intelligence.

2. Discuss the characteristics of a psychological test.

3. Describe the Stanford-Binet Intelligence Scale, explaining the three-level hierarchical model of cognitive ability and the notion of intelligence quotient.

4. Describe the Wechsler Intelligence Scales.

5. Discuss the controversy about the quality of individual intelligence tests.

6. Distinguish the specific skills and abilities that appear to be gender driven.

7. Explain the different methods used to study age effects on IQ and the different results obtained from the two methods.

8. Discuss how fluid and crystallized intelligence are affected by age.

9. Summarize the data on racial differences in IQ scores and arguments about the causes of such differences.

10. List six ways in which individuals can be considered gifted.

11. Define mental retardation.

12. Discuss some of the causes of mental retardation.

I.   Just What is Intelligence?

    A.   Two definitions of intelligence cover both theoretical and practical considerations.
        1.   David Wechsler defined intelligence as the capacity to understand the world and the resourcefulness to cope with its challenges.
        2.   E. G. Boring provided an operational definition of intelligence: intelligence is what is measured by intelligence tests.
    B.   Psychologists have conceptualized intelligence in various ways.
        1.   Charles Spearman believed intelligence consists of two factors: a general intelligence, called a g-factor and an s-factor consisting of a collection of specific cognitive skills.
        2.   L. L. Thurstone found no support for a g-factor of intelligence, arguing instead that intellectual ability falls into seven primary mental abilities.
        3.   J. P. Guilford complicated matters by claiming that intelligence can be analyzed as three intersecting dimensions: the *mental operations* involved in the task, the *content* of the material used, and the *product* of the task.
        4.   Phillip Vernon proposed a hierarchy of intellectual skills and abilities that combines some of the thinking of the above three theorists.
    C.   Contemporary theories of intelligence take a different approach than earlier theories.
        1.   Robert Sternberg's tricomponent theory of intelligence proposes a componential intelligence, an experiential intelligence, and a contextual intelligence, only the first of which is measured on standard intelligence tests.
        2.   Howard Gardner proposes that intelligence can be displayed in any one of seven ways.
    D.   No model of intelligence has been tested fully enough to determine the extent to which it accurately characterizes human intelligence.

II.   Psychological Tests of Intelligence

    A.   A psychological test is an objective, standardized measure of a sample of behavior.
    B.   The quality of a psychological test depends on the extent to which it has three characteristics: reliability, validity, and adequate norms.
    C.   The Stanford-Binet Intelligence Scale, initially the work of Alfred Binet but later translated and revised by Lewis Terman, calculated an intelligent quotient (IQ): the mental age level (or MA) determined by the test was divided by a subject's chronological age to find the IQ.
    D.   The Wechsler Adult Intelligence Scale (WAIS) was developed for use with adult populations and to reduce the heavy reliance on verbal skills found in the old versions of the Stanford-Binet; it is the most commonly used of all psychological tests.
        1.   The Wechsler Scale for Children (WISC-R) is for ages 6 to 17; the Wechsler Preschool and Primary Scale of Intelligence (WPPSI) is for ages 4 to 6 1/2.
        2.   Wechsler tests provide one overall score plus independent verbal and performance scores.
    E.   There has been much controversy surrounding individually administered intelligence tests, e.g., are the tests culturally biased, or do they truly measure intelligence.
    F.   Group intelligence tests, which can be administered to large numbers at once and are usually paper-and-pencil tests, were developed to overcome a major disadvantage of individual tests.
    G.   Aptitude tests, such as the ACT and SAT, are psychological tests of cognitive ability that are used to predict future behaviors.

III.   Group Differences in Measured Intelligence

    A.   Measured intelligence, in this context, refers to one's IQ score and should not be equated with one's intelligence.
    B.   Demonstrating significant differences in IQ scores between two groups tells nothing about why the differences exists, nor does it allow for definitive statements about individual members of the groups.
    C.   There is little support for gender differences on any test represented by an IQ score.
    D.   Beyond global measures of IQ, we find signs of gender differences on specific intellectual skills.
        1.   Males score significantly higher than females on tests of spatial relations.
        2.   A recent study found that males scored higher on math and science tests, but females scored better than males on perceptual speed, reading comprehension, and writing skills tests.

E. Researchers are also interested in the relationship between age and IQ.
  1. IQ test scores of children younger than seven are poor predictors of IQ in later life.
  2. Cross-sectional research methods indicate IQ peaks in the early twenties, stabilizes for about twenty years, then declines rapidly; however, studies using the longitudinal method show IQ scores rise until the mid-fifties, after which they decline very gradually.
  3. Specific intellectual skills do not decline at the same rate, and some don't decline at all.
  4. Abilities related to fluid intelligence show the greatest impairment with age; abilities depending on crystallized intelligence remain constant or even increase over the life span.
F. Researchers have also been curious about racial and ethnic differences in IQ; certain findings have been consistent, but the reasons behind them are currently largely undetermined.

IV. Extremes of Intelligence

A. The most frequently occurring score is the average IQ of 100; about 95 percent of all IQ scores fall between 70 and 130.
B. The mentally gifted are people whose IQ scores are above 130 (less than 3 percent of the population) , and there are many ways in which a person can be mentally gifted, e.g., psychomotor ability or leadership ability.
C. Mental retardation is defined as "subaverage general intellectual functioning which originated during the developmental period and is associated with impairment in adaptive functioning"; retardation is categorized into four major degrees, and it's estimated that about 3 percent of the population fall within the IQ range for retardation.
D. Psychologists suspect there are hundreds of causes of mental retardation, including problems that develop before, during, or just after birth, Down syndrome (caused by an extra 47th chromosome), and Fragile X Syndrome.

TOPIC 7B – Language and Problem Solving

Learning Objectives – Language

1. Explain psycholinguistics.

2. List the defining characteristics of language.

3. Discuss how pragmatics are related to social context.

4. Describe the landmark events that occur during language acquisition.

5. Discuss how researchers determine how language is acquired.

6. What evidence exists to support or refute theories of language acquisition?

7. Explain why an interactionist approach to language acquisition is more feasible.

8. List three components of a problem.

9. Explain how to distinguish problems that are well defined or ill defined.

10. Describe problem representation.

11. Discuss how algorithmic and heuristic strategies are used to solve problems.

12. Define mental set and explain how it affects problem solving.

13. Explain functional fixedness, and describe its effects on problem solving.

14. Contrast divergent thinking and convergent thinking.

15. List and explain the four stages of creative problem solving.

I.   Language

   A. Language is a large collection of arbitrary symbols (words) that have significance for a language-using community and that follow certain rules of combination.
   B. Psycholinguistics, a hybrid discipline, consists of scientists trained in psychology and linguistics who analyze language, usually at three levels.
       1. Phonemes are the individual speech sounds of a language; English has approximately 45 phonemes.
       2. Semantics refers to the study of the meaning of a language.
       3. Syntax refers to the rules that govern how sentences are formed.
   C. Pragmatics is the study of how linguistic events are related to the social context in which they occur.

II. Language Acquisition

   A. Language acquisition, the process of developing each facet of language, is one of the most significant achievements of childhood.
       1. At about 6 months, random cries of infants are replaced with babbling, which occurs for all babies in the same way crossculturally–even for deaf infants.
       2. Children comprehend or understand speech before they can produce it, and they use language in a rule-governed way, though they do not use the same rules as adults.
       3. The first use of vocalization as language is called holophrastic speech, followed by the appearance of two-word utterances at about 2 years.
       4. Next, there is a period typified by telegraphic speech comprised of nouns, verbs, and adjectives.
       5. At about age five, children demonstrate both the understanding and the production of virtually every type of acceptable sentence structure in language.
   B. Some language acquisition can be accounted for by learning, while other aspects suggest a biological basis; a language acquisition device has been proposed as the biological mechanism.
   C. An interactionist approach incorporating an innate, biological, predisposition to acquire language with experiences in a language-using community is currently most feasible.

III. Problem Solving

   A. A problem occurs when there is a discrepancy between the present state and the perceived goal state and no clear way exists for getting from one to the other.
   B. A problem has three components: an initial state, a goal state, and possible routes or strategies for getting from the initial state to the goal state.
   C. The problem must first be represented in our minds, but this often provides the main stumbling block to problem solution.
   D. A problem solving strategy is a systematic plan for generating possible solutions that can be tested to see if they are correct; cognitive strategies, algorithms, and heuristic strategies are examples.

IV. Barriers to Effective Problem Solving

   A. Mental set is a tendency to perceive or respond to something in a given (set) way.
   B. Functional fixedness is an inability to discover an appropriate new use for an object because of experience using the object for some typical function.
   C. Sometimes heuristic problem solving strategies are biased because of perceptions of past experience, and thus they create a barrier to effective problem solving.
   D. The restraints imposed by improper mental sets, functional fixedness, and some heuristic strategies must be overcome for effective problem solving to occur.
   E. Creative solutions to overcoming problem solving barriers usually involve new and different organization of problem elements.
       1. Divergent thinking starts with one idea and from it generates a large number of alternative possibilities; it is generally more useful in creative problem solving.
       2. Convergent thinking takes many different ideas and tries to focus and reduce them to just one possible solution.
       3. Creative problem solving can be divided into four interrelated stages: preparation, incubation, illumination, and verification.

CHAPTER 8

HUMAN DEVELOPMENT

TOPIC 8A – The Development of Children

Learning Objectives–Prenatal Development

1. Summarize the stage of the zygote in prenatal development.

2. Discuss the embryonic stage of development, including cell differentiation and environmental sensitivity.

3. Explain the fetal stage of prenatal development.

4. Discuss the adverse effects of poor diet during pregnancy.

5. Describe the impact of drugs and stress on prenatal development and birth.

6. Explain the role of the father in prenatal development.

7. Define reflexes, and discuss their importance.

8. Explain the newborn's sensory and perceptual abilities.

9. Describe the cognitive skills that develop during each of Piaget's cognitive stages.

10. Discuss the criticisms of Piaget's theory.

11. Explain Kohlberg's theory of moral development.

12. Discuss criticisms of Kohlberg's theory.

13. Describe Erikson's childhood stages of development.

14. Explain the development of gender identity and its effects on social development.

15. Discuss the importance of attachment.

I. The Stages of Prenatal Development

    A. Human development begins at conception when the father's sperm cell unites with the mother's ovum and twenty-three chromosomes from each parent pair off within a single cell, the zygote.

    B. The period from conception to birth, the prenatal period, is divided into three stages: the zygote stage, the stage of the embryo, and the stage of the fetus–the longest stage.

II. Environmental Influences On Prenatal Development

    A. During the rapid stage of prenatal development, even small environmental disturbances can have serious and lasting consequences.

    B. Maternal malnutrition often leads to increases in miscarriages, stillbirths, and premature births.

    C. Many drugs and chemicals affect the developing organism; smoking, heavy drinking, and psychoactive drugs have been shown to have serious effects on the unborn.

    D. The role of the father in prenatal development is just beginning to be assessed.
        1. Only one percent of the 577 studies cited in a review of the literature focuses on the father's role.
        2. The age of the father, as well as the mother, appears to matter.

III. Motor Development: Getting From Here to There

    A. Through the first two weeks of life the newborn is referred to as a neonate, and neonates are capable of a wide range of mostly reflexive behaviors; more than a dozen reflexes can be observed and measured.

    B. In their first three years, children experience a growth rate never duplicated, and the sequencing is predictable.
        1. Cephalocaudal sequencing refers to the fact that a child's growth and bodily control proceed from head to lower body.
        2. Proximodistal sequencing refers to the fact that growth and bodily control in children proceed from the center core to the extremities.

IV. Sensory and Perceptual Development

    A. Infants can focus on objects at one or two feet.

    B. Newborns react to depth by closing their eyes and squirming away if an object is rushed toward their face.

    C. Neonates can demonstrate sound localization, and they respond differently to different pitches and loudness.

    D. Newborns can discriminate between the four basic taste qualities, preferring sweet-tasting liquids.

V. Cognitive and Social Development

    A. Neonates can engage in simple learning tasks.

    B. Other cognitive abilities have been demonstrated in newborns, such as memory, facial recognition, and discrimination among facially expressed emotions.

    C. Piaget's theory of cognitive development centers on acquiring schemas, or organized mental representations of the world.
        1. Organizing and forming mental representations involves two basic processes: assimilation and accommodation.
        2. Piaget proposed that children progress through four stages of development as they assimilate and accommodate: the sensorimotor stage, the preoperational stage, the concrete operations stage, and the formal operations stage.

    D. Some research has challenged Piaget's basic ideas and has found a few discrepancies.

    E. Lawrence Kohlberg developed a stage theory of moral development consisting of three levels: the preconventional level, the conventional level, and the postconventional level.
        1. To varying degrees, Kohlberg's descriptions are valid for several cultures.
        2. The theory has some problems, however; not all people develop the higher stages of moral reasoning nor, argues Gilligan, is girls' moral reasoning consistent with boys' moral reasoning.

    F. Erik Erikson proposed a psychosocial, stage theory of development listing eight stages, where each stage consists of a series of conflicts or crises that must be resolved.

G. The development of gender identity, one's sense of maleness or femaleness, is an important part of a child's development.
   1. Differences between male and female infants and children turn out to be few and subtle.
   2. The only area in which North American parents significantly differentiate between boys and girls is in the encouragement of different sex-typed activities.
   3. Peer groups provide important experiences for both sexes.
   4. By school age most children associate particular personality traits with men and women, that is, they develop their gender identify.
   5. Cognitive psychologists suggest that children's ability to discriminate between the sexes facilitates development of schemas for gender-related information.
H. Attachment is defined as a strong, two-way emotional bond, usually referring to the relationship between a child and his or her mother or primary caregiver.
   1. Strong attachments are most likely to be formed if the mother is sensitive to the needs of the child.
   2. Around 65 percent of American children are securely attached by one year of age.
   3. Secure attachment in infancy leads to sociability, higher self-esteem, better relationships with siblings, and fewer aggressive behaviors, better classroom behavior, and more empathy for others.
   4. Infants can and do form attachments with their fathers.
   5. The most important factor in determining the overall benefit of day care is the quality of care the children receive, no matter where they receive it.

TOPIC 8B – Development in Adolescence and Adulthood

1. Define adolescence and characterize this developmental period.

2. Describe the physical changes that accompany adolescence.

3. Summarize the adolescent's search for identity as described by Erikson.

4. Discuss drug use and abuse in adolescence.

5. Describe sexuality in adolescence, and explain the associated problem of teenage pregnancy.

6. Describe the characteristic developments of early adulthood.

7. Summarize the issues that are typically faced during middle adulthood.

8. Describe the elderly population in the United States and the problems associated with ageism.

9. Discuss Kübler-Ross's theory of death and dying and its criticisms.

I. What Are Adolescents Really Like?

   A. Adolescence is a developmental period of transition between childhood dependence to adult independence that has biological, psychological, and social implications.
   B. Adolescence may be characterized as a period of turmoil, stress, and rebellion, but over the past 25 years it has come to be regarded more as a time of personal growth, independence and positive change.

II. Some of the Challenges of Adolescence

   A. At the onset of adolescence there is a marked increase in height and weight known as the growth spurt, as well as sexual maturation, which is accompanied by an increase in the production of sex hormones.
   B. The major task of adolescence is the resolution of an identity crisis, which revolves around the struggle to define and integrate the sense of who one is, what one is to do in life, and what one's attitudes, beliefs, and values should be.
      1. The concept of identity formation is associated with the personality theorist, Erik Erikson.
      2. Role confusion may result from perceived societal pressures on adolescents to decide what they want to be when they grow up.
   C. Many adolescents experiment with using drugs–particularly smoking (79 percent) and drinking alcohol (65 percent); many use drugs on a regular basis, and many abuse drugs.
   D. During adolescence, large doses of sex hormones enter the bloodstream and stimulate the development of secondary sex characteristics, and many teens become sexually active.
      1. The CDC reports premarital activity among adolescent females has almost doubled during the last two decades from 28.6% in 1970 to 51.5% in 1988.
      2. Teenage pregnancy has surfaced as a major social problem in the United States because each year more than half a million babies are born to adolescent mothers, and approximately 400,000 teenage pregnancies end in abortion each year.
   E. Adolescence is a period of challenge and perhaps risk and danger, but it also represents the opportunity for growth, newfound freedom, responsibility, and independence.

III. Early Adulthood

   A. Adulthood can be considered in terms of three overlapping periods: early adulthood, middle adulthood, and late adulthood.
   B. Two important decision-making processes during early adulthood are the choice of a mate and family and the choice of job or career.
      1. Erikson described the conflict of early adulthood as intimacy vs. isolation.
      2. Similar people, not opposites, are more likely to attract us, particularly on such dimensions as age, education, race, religion, and ethnic background.
      3. Men and women are in agreement about the characteristics they prefer in a mate, differing only on good earning potential (women rate higher) and physical attractiveness (men rate higher).
      4. Choice of marriage partners is not always based on rationality; romantic love or economic hardships often play a part.
      5. Becoming a parent is often taken as a sure sign of adulthood, and according to Erikson, having a family fosters the process of generativity–a concern for family and for one's impact on future generations.
   C. One's occupational choice and satisfaction with that choice affects one's self-esteem and identity; employment outside the home is a major determinant of self-worth and satisfaction for women.
      1. Dual career families are becoming quite common; women now constitute about 39 percent of the professional labor force in the U. S.
      2. Career choice involves seven stages: exploration, crystallization, choice, career clarification, induction, reformation, and integration.

IV. Middle Adulthood

    A. Most people's place in the framework of society is fairly well set by the time they are 40.
    B. Several significant tasks may present themselves in middle adulthood.
        1. People are adjusting to the physiological changes of middle age.
        2. Reaching and maintaining satisfactory performance in their occupations is relevant here.
        3. People are working at achieving adult social and civic responsibility, relating to their spouses as a person, and developing leisure-time activities.

V. Late Adulthood

    A. More than 30.4 million Americans were in their early to mid-60s in 1988; by 2050 persons aged 65 and over are predicted to number 78.9 million, with an average life span of 82.1 years.
    B. Ageism refers to the discrimination or negative stereotypes that are formed on the basis of age.
    C. It is a misconception about the aged that they live in misery: most welcome retirement, and a 1981 poll found only 31 percent of respondents over 65 claimed poor health to be a serious problem.
    D. Developmental psychologists find it useful to divide those over 65 into groups of young-old and old-old.
        1. This distinction is made on the basis of psychological, social, and health characteristics.
        2. The young-old group forms the large majority, 80 to 85 percent.
    E. Most research on the elderly has focused on average age-related losses; the concept of successful aging has only recently gotten attention.
    F. Dealing with our own death is the last major crisis we face in life.

CHAPTER 9

PERSONALITY

TOPIC 9A – Theories of Personality

Learning Objectives

1. Discuss the three levels of consciousness proposed by Freud.

2. List Freud's three structures of personality and the principles by which they operate.

3. Describe Freudian defense mechanisms and their purposes.

4. Summarize Freud's psychosexual stages of development.

5. Explain the contributions of Adler, Jung, and Horney to the psychoanalytic approach.

6. Describe the personality theories of Watson, Skinner, Dollard and Miller, and Bandura.

7. Discuss the humanistic approach to personality theorized by Rogers and Maslow.

8. Define personality trait.

9. List the "Big Five" personality dimensions.

10. Discuss the strengths and weaknesses of the psychoanalytic, humanistic, trait, and behaviorist approaches to personality.

I. Preview

    A. A theory is an organized collection of testable ideas used to explain a particular subject matter.

    B. Personality includes the affects, behaviors and cognitions (ABCs) of people that characterize them in many situations over time.

    C. Personality theories look for ways to describe how individuals remain the same over time and circumstances and to allow for description of differences that exist among people.

    D. Personality somehow resides inside the person; it's something a person brings to his or her interactions with the environment.

II. The Psychoanalytic Approach

    A. The psychoanalytic approach, which is associated with Sigmund Freud and his students, relies on innate, inborn drives as explanatory concepts of human behavior and accepts the power and influence of the unconscious.

    B. Freud's approach in therapy and his theories about the nature of personality arose largely from observations of his patients and intensive self-examination.

    C. Freud believed there are three levels of consciousness: the conscious, the preconscious, and the unconscious.

    D. According to Freudian theory, our goal in life is to resolve conflicts between two basic instincts: life instincts (eros) and death instincts (thanatos).

    E. Freud also proposed that the human personality is composed of three separate, though interacting, structures or subsystems: the id operates on the pleasure principle and resides in the unconscious, the ego operates on the reality principle, and the superego operates on the idealistic principle and has no contact with reality.

    F. Freud (1856-1939) suggested a psychosexual stage theory of the development of personality.

        1. In the oral stage (birth to one year), the child derives pleasure from oral activities: feeding, sucking, and making noises.

        2. In the anal stage (ages 1 to 3 years), children develop the ability to control their bowel and bladder habits and can display aggression by either "going" at inappropriate times or refusing to "go" when placed on the potty chair.

        3. In the phallic stage (ages 3 to 5 years), the genitals replace the mouth as the child's source of pleasure; it is at this stage that the Oedipus complex (boys) or Electra complex (girls) develops.

        4. During the stage of latency (ages 4 to 6), sexual development is on hold as the ego develops.

        5. The genital stage (from puberty on) involves a sexual reawakening and renewal of sexual impulses.

    G. Neo-Freudians were bothered by the focus on biological instincts and libido and the lack of concern for social influences.

        1. Alfred Adler (1870-1937) proposed that we are very much products of the social influences on our personalities and that our major goal is the achievement of success or superiority.

        2. Carl Jung (1875-1961) believed our major goal in life is unity with all the aspects of our personality, and he proposed a collective unconscious that contains archetypes, or universal forms and patterns of thought.

        3. Karen Horney (1885-1952) placed great emphasis on early childhood experiences, and was the first to take Freud's theories to task over their male bias.

    H. The psychoanalytic approach, particularly as modified by the neo-Freudians, is the most comprehensive and complex of the personality theories and has several positive aspects, but there also remain criticisms of Freudian psychoanalytic theory.

III. The Behavioral-Learning Approach

    A. John Watson (1878-1958) and his followers argued that psychology should turn away from the study of the mind and consciousness because they are unverifiable and ultimately unscientific, and should study only observable behavior and the role of the environment in shaping behaviors.

    B. B. F. Skinner (1904-1990) refused to refer to any sort of internal variables to explain behavior; he believed behaviors that result in reinforcement are repeated and those not reinforced tend not to be repeated.

    C. John Dollard (1900-1980) and Neal Miller (b. 1909) tried to use the basic principles of learning theory, such as habits and drives, to explain personality and how it develops.

D. Albert Bandura (b. 1925) proposes that learning involves a cognitive rearrangement and representation, not just a series of stimulus-response activities and that many aspects of our behavior are learned through observation and social influence.
E. The behavioral/learning approach also has its weaknesses and strengths.
   1. Some argue that this approach totally dehumanizes personality.
   2. They tend not to be theories at all, at least not very comprehensive theories.
   3. To their credit, theorists using this approach demand that theoretical terms be carefully defined and that hypotheses be verified experimentally.

IV. The Humanistic-Phenomenological Approach

A. This approach to personality contrasts with both the psychoanalytic and behavioral approaches in that it is not deterministic, it tends to focus much more on the here and now, and it tends to emphasize the wholeness or completeness of the personality.
B. Carl Rogers's (1902-1986) view of personality, referred to as person-centered theory, holds that the most powerful of human drives is the drive to become fully functioning.
C. Abraham Maslow (1908-1970) saw as our major goal in life the need to realize positive needs, to self-actualize.
D. The humanistic-phenomenological approach reminds us of the wholeness of the personality and warns us of the danger in analyzing personality in artificial segments, but it is almost impossible to test any of its assumptions scientifically because terms are fuzzy and ill-defined.

V. The Trait Approach

A. Theories about traits, which are relatively enduring way in which one individual differs from others, tend to be more concerned with the adequate description of personality than with the explanation of personality.
B. The main issue for trait psychologists is to determine which traits are important, which dimensions best characterize people, and how these differ from other dimensions.
C. Gordon Allport (1897-1967) proposed that personality traits are of two types: common traits, which are shared by almost everyone and personal dispositions, which include cardinal traits, central traits, and secondary traits.
D. Raymond Cattell (b. 1905) proposed a technique for analyzing personality traits (consisting of surface traits and source traits) that relies on the results of psychological tests, questionnaires, surveys, and a statistical technique called factor analysis.
E. The five-factor model is the contemporary model consisting of the traits which most research supports as descriptors of personality.
   1. The five dimensions are extroversion/introversion, agreeableness or friendliness, conscientiousness, emotionality, and intelligence.
   2. Each trait represents a dimension of possible habits and individual responses that a person may bring to bear in any given situation.
F. Trait theories provide us with descriptive terms and an idea of how measured traits are related to one another, but they offer little more than description and not all agree on which traits are the most important.

TOPIC 9B – Issues Related to Personality

Learning Objectives

1. Summarize the debate concerning personality versus situational influences on behavior.

2. Discuss what we know about gender differences in personality traits.

3. Explain how behavioral observations are used for assessing personality.

4. Discuss the advantages and disadvantages of the interview as a personality assessment technique.

5. Describe the MMPI-2, and define multiphasic.

6. Explain how the MMPI-2 was constructed.

7. Explain how the California Personality Inventory differs from the MMPI.

8. Discuss differences between the Taylor Manifest Anxiety Scale and the Endler Multidimensional Anxiety Scale.

9. Describe the characteristics of projective techniques.

10. Explain the Rorschach and the TAT, and discuss their reliability and validity.

I.   Is There a Personality?

   A. Theoretical approaches to personality all address the consistency of personality, but in 1968 Walter Michel challenged the assumption of consistency of personality.
   B. Methodology borrowed from behavioral genetics argues that behavior does reflect individual differences more than situational factors.
   C. In general, personality theorists today take an interactionist approach; how one behaves is a function of an interaction of stable personality characteristics and the individual's perception of the situation.

II.   Gender and Personality

   A. Eleanor Maccoby and Carol Jacklin did the first large-scale studies on gender differences in personality.
   B. Later research has confirmed that gender differences tend to be insignificant and inconsistent.
   C. One glaring exception to this research is that males have been found to be consistently more physically aggressive than females.
      1. This difference seems to be at all ages and in all cultural settings.
      2. However, "averages" don't preclude any one female being significantly more aggressive than any one male, and we have no evidence that this difference is necessarily genetic or biologically based.
   D. Small gender differences have occasionally been found in other areas, including communication style, decoding or interpreting body language, and self-confidence.

III. Personality Measurement or Assessment

   A. The key to personality assessment is to reliably and validly measure personal characteristics.
   B. Adequate diagnosis, theory building, and prediction of behavior are three goals behind personality measurement.
   C. Behavioral observation involves drawing conclusions about an individual's personality on the basis of observations of his or her behavior.
      1. There may be problems with behavioral observations, but they can be an excellent source of information, particularly when the observations being made are purposeful, careful, and structured.
      2. Behavioral observations are commonly a part of any clinical assessment, and may include role-playing.
      3. Observational techniques may be supplemented with rating scales, which provide many advantages over casual observation.
   D. Interviews involve a conversational interchange between the interviewer and the subject to gain information about the subject.
      1. The basic idea of the interview is to focus on what people say about themselves rather than what they do.
      2. There is little evidence that unstructured interviews have much reliability or validity; structured interviews compensate for this lack.
   E. There are several varieties of paper and pencil personality tests.
      1. The MMPI, the most researched test in psychology and one of the most commonly used, is a pencil-and-paper test used to assess a number of personality dimensions; it was originally designed to help in the diagnosis of persons with mental disturbances.
      2. The California Personality Inventory (CPI) was constructed with the same logic as the MMPI using only normal subjects.
      3. The 16 PF (PF stands for personality factors) Questionnaire is a multiphasic test that was designed around Cattell's trait theory.
      4. The Taylor Manifest Anxiety Scale is an inventory designed to measure just one trait, and thus is not multiphasic.
      5. The Endler Multidimensional Anxiety Scale purports to distinguish between anxiety and depression.
   F. Projective techniques are personality assessment techniques requiring subjects to respond to ambiguous stimuli, thus "projecting" some of their "selves" into their responses.
      1. The Rorschach inkblot test is a famous projective technique in which the subject is asked to say what is seen in a series of inkblots, but it is neither very reliable nor valid.
      2. Some formal scoring schemes are available for the Thematic Apperception Test, a projective technique in which subjects are asked to tell a story about a set of ambiguous pictures, but scoring and interpretation are usually quite subjective.

CHAPTER 10

MOTIVATION AND EMOTION

TOPIC 10A – Issues of Motivation

Learning Objectives

1. Discuss how instinct, drive, and incentive have been used to explain motivated behaviors.

2. Explain how the concept of balance or equilibrium can be used to explain motivated behaviors.

3. Describe how homeostasis relates to temperature regulation as a physiologically based drive.

4. List the factors that may influence thirst and hunger.

5. Describe the symptoms of anorexia nervosa and bulimia, and explain the prognosis for each disorder.

6. Discuss the ways in which the sex drive is a unique, physiologically based drive.

7. Explain the male and female sexual dysfunctions and their causes.

8. Discuss homosexuality, including characteristics and potential causes.

9. Discuss achievement motivation and explain how it is measured.

10. Discuss the need for power and the need for affiliation.

I.   How Shall We Characterize Motivation?

   A.   Motivation is defined as the process that arouses, directs, and maintains behavior.
   B.   No one approach to motivation answers all our questions about why organisms do what they do.
   C.   In the early days of psychology, behaviors were often explained in terms of innate instincts.
   D.   An alternative explanation referred to needs and drives; instincts are tied to specific patterns of behavior; needs and drives are not.
      1.   Clark Hull defined a need as a shortage or lack of some biological essential required for survival.
      2.   A drive is a state of tension, arousal, or activation that organisms seek to reduce.
   E.   To claim that drives arise only from needs that derive from biological deprivations seems unduly restrictive, and this explanation does not account for behaviors engaged in even after all biological needs are met.
   F.   Abraham Maslow believed needs that ultimately motivate human action are limited in number, are not always physiological, and are hierarchically arranged; he developed a stage theory based on this hierarchy of needs.
   G.   One alternative to a drive reduction approach focuses on the end state, or goal, of behavior, not needs or drives within the organism.
   H.   The basic idea of approaches based on balance or equilibrium is that we are motivated to maintain a state of balance, or homeostasis.
      1.   Arousal theories of motivation claim there is an optimal level of arousal that organisms are motivated to maintain.
      2.   Optimum levels of arousal vary with the nature or difficulty or complexity of the task, and may vary considerably from individual to individual.

II.   Temperature Regulation

   A.   The term *drive* is used for activators and directors of behavior that have known biological bases; the term *motive* refers to those that do not.
   B.   Whenever anything happens to elevate or depress our body temperature above or below its homeostatic level, we become motivated.
      1.   Two centers in the hypothalamus act together as a thermostat: one is sensitive to elevated body temperatures, and one is sensitive to lowered temperatures.
      2.   When automatic physiological reactions are not successful, some voluntary action may be taken.

III.   The Thirst Drive and Drinking Behaviors

   A.   About two-thirds of the fluid in our bodies is contained within our bodies' cells (intracellular); one third is held in the spaces between cells (extracellular).
      1.   Intercellular loss of fluid is monitored by regions of the hypothalamus.
      2.   Extracellular fluid loss is also monitored in the brain, but involves the kidneys as well.
   B.   External, psychological cues may also influence drinking behavior.

IV.   The Hunger Drive and Eating Behaviors

   A.   Internal, physiological cues that motivate a person to feel hungry and eat originate in the hypothalamus and the liver, although glucose and levels of stored fat have also been implicated.
      1.   The concept of homeostasis suggests a person's overall body weight is physiologically regulated, so that if body weight decreases significantly, the organism is driven to return to the set point level.
      2.   Research on twins suggests that genetic forces work to determine one's overall body size and fat distribution.
      3.   Recently researchers announced the isolation of an obese gene, but we do not yet know the long-term results of these discoveries.
   B.   We often respond to external cues that stimulate us to engage in eating behavior, such as the stimulus properties of food, or habit, or we may eat simply because others around us are eating.

C. Occasionally, a concern about becoming overweight can lead to seriously maladjusted behaviors, called eating disorders.
   1. Anorexia nervosa is characterized by the reduction of body weight through self-starvation and/or increased activity; the prognosis for anorexia nervosa is poor.
   2. Bulimia is an eating disorder characterized by recurrent episodes of binge eating and then purging to remove the just-eaten food; the prognosis for bulimia is better.

V. The Sex Drive and Human Sexual Behaviors

   A. As a physiologically based drive, the sex drive is unique in several ways, e.g., survival of the individual does not depend on its satisfaction, or it is not present at birth, but requires maturation.
   B. Sexual dysfunction is the name given to any chronic problem, disturbance, or inadequacy of sexual functioning.
      1. It is difficult to determine the number of persons experiencing sexual dsyfunctions, primarily because of people's unwillingness to discuss them.
      2. Two common dsyfunctions in men are erectile dysfunction and premature ejaculation; retarded ejaculation is less common.
      3. Three sexual dysfunctions experienced by women are female sexual unresponsiveness, orgasmic dysfunction, and vaginismus.
      4. Most sexual dysfunctions are amenable to treatment and therapy, and there are preventative steps that can be taken.
   C. Homosexuals are individuals who are sexually attracted to and aroused by members of their own sex.
      1. Psychologists agree that homosexuality and heterosexuality are not mutually exclusive categories.
      2. Conservative estimates suggest that about two percent of American males are exclusively homosexual; female homosexuality is approximately half as prevalent as male homosexuality.
      3. Sexual preference does not distinguish patterns of sexual responsiveness.
      4. There is no generally accepted theory about the causes of homosexuality.

VI. Psychologically Based Motives

   A. Achievement motivation is defined as the acquired need to meet or exceed some standard of success or excellence in one's behaviors, and it is usually assessed by use of the TAT.
      1. McClelland found consistent differences between those with high need for achievement and those without it.
      2. High achievement people aren't always interested in their success alone; particularly in collectivist societies, people with high need for achievement may work very hard to achieve goals only available to the group.
   B. Power motivation consists of a need to be in control of both the situation and of others, and is also measured using the TAT.
   C. Affiliation motivation involves a need to be with others, to work with others, and to form friendships and associations.
      1. This need is usually at odds with a need for power.
      2. Affiliation and achievement needs are reasonably independent.
      3. Affiliation needs may be at least partly biologically based.

TOPIC 10B – The Psychology of Emotion

Learning Objectives

1. List four components that define emotional experience.

2. Discuss the controversy surrounding the search for basic, or primary, emotions.

3. Describe the activities of the sympathetic division of the autonomic nervous system during states of emotionality.

4. Describe the various brain centers that are involved in emotionality.

5. Discuss the relationship between facial expressions and emotion.

6. List the facial expressions universally recognized.

I.   Defining and Classifying Emotions

A. In defining emotion, one must look at four interactive components: a subjective feeling which may be labeled, the cognitive reaction, the physiological reaction involving glands, hormones, and internal organs, and an overt behavioral reaction.

B. Several researchers have attempted to develop a scheme, or plan, to describe and classify emotions in a systematic way.
1. Wilhelm Wundt believed emotions could be described in terms of three intersecting dimensions: pleasantness-unpleasantness, relaxation-tension, and calm-excitement.
2. Carroll Izard proposed nine primary emotions, from which all others could be constructed: fear, anger, shame, contempt, disgust, distress, interest, surprise and joy.
3. Robert Plutchik argued for eight primary basic emotions because each could be directly tied to some adaptive pattern (related to survival) of behavior.
4. Richard Lazarus proposed a new theory stressing the motivational role of emotionality and proposing fifteen primary emotions, each with a relational theme.

C. None of the approaches to classifying emotions has proven completely satisfactory; the only issue on which there seems to be consensus is that emotions are valenced states.

II.   Physiological Aspects of Emotion

A. The autonomic nervous system, which consists of two parts, is primarily involved in emotional responses.
1. The parasympathetic division is actively involved in maintaining a relaxed, calm, and unemotional state.
2. The sympathetic division is responsible for physiological responses to stress, such as dilated pupils, elevated heart rate and blood pressure, and increased respiration and blood sugar levels.

B. The brain, primarily the limbic system and the hypothalamus, ultimately controls all emotional responses.
1. Exactly how the limbic system and the hypothalamus coordinate emotion is not yet understood.
2. The cerebral cortex modifies emotional reactions and controls the cognitive aspect of emotion by the interpretation of, and memory for, emotional events.

III. Outward Expressions of Emotion

A   Language and facial expression are important ways of displaying emotions.
1. Nonhuman animals have many ritualistic, complex, and instinctive patterns of behavior to communicate many emotional states.
2. Body language can also communicate emotional condition through postural cues and gestures.

B. A growing body of evidence supports the idea that facial expressions of some of the basic emotional states (fear, happiness, disgust, surprise, anger, and sadness) may be innate responses.
1. Several studies by Paul Ekman and his colleagues demonstrate a reliable relationship between emotional state and facial expression cross-culturally.
2. A follow-up study by Ekman showed that simply moving one's facial muscles into positions associated with emotional expression can actually cause distinctive physiological changes associated with that emotional state.

CHAPTER 11

PSYCHOLOGY, STRESS, AND PHYSICAL HEALTH

TOPIC 11A – Stress, Stressors, and How to Cope

Learning Objectives

1. Define stress and stressors.

2. Define frustration-induced stress.

3. Name four types of motivational conflict and give an example of each.

4. Discuss the SRRS and the Hassle Scale as measures of the stress of everyday life.

5. Discuss individual differences in reaction to stressors; identify the characteristics of the hardy personality.

6. Name and describe the three stages of Selye's general adaptation syndrome.

7. List and discuss eight effective strategies for coping with stress.

8. Explain three ineffective strategies for coping with stress.

I.   Stressors: The Causes of Stress

    A. Stress is defined as a complex set of reactions made as a response to a perceived threat to one's well-being, such as frustration, conflict, and life events, that includes physiological reactions and unpleasant feelings.

    B. Stress is not necessarily a response to some overwhelming, catastrophic event; trivial events can cause stress also.

    C. Behind the study of frustration-induced stress is the assumption that all behavior is goal directed, and frustration is the blocking of goal-directed behavior.

    D. Conflict-induced stress arises when we are unable to satisfy a particular drive or motive because it is in conflict with other motives that are influencing us at the same time.

        1. Approach-approach conflicts produce the least amount of stress because the organism is caught between two potentially desirable alternatives.

        2. Avoidance-avoidance conflicts are characterized by two alternatives, each of which is negative or punishing.

        3. Approach-avoidance conflicts are typified by vacillation between being motivated to approach and motivated to avoid a particular goal.

        4. Multiple approach-avoidance conflicts arise when an individual is faced with a number of alternatives, each of which is in some way positive and negative at the same time.

    E. Sources of stress that do not fit neatly into our descriptions of either conflict or frustration are called life-induced stress.

        1. Socioeconomic status (SES), a measure reflecting one's income, educational level, and occupation, is positively related to experienced stress.

        2. Richard Lazarus argues that big crises or major events are often too large to have an impact on us directly; what may cause us to feel stressed are the ways in which these big events produce little changes in our lives.

II.   Reacting to the Stressors in Our Lives

    A. There are large variances between how people perceive stressful situations and how they respond to them.

    B. Some people, labeled as having "hardy personalities," seem to be very resistant to the negative effects of stress because they view stressful situations as opportunity for growth, are optimistic and feel in control of their own lives, and are committed to, and involved in, life.

    C. Selye's description of the general adaptation syndrome (GAS) is the most widely accepted description of the physiological reactions to stressors.

        1. The GAS occurs in three stages: the alarm state where heart rate and blood pressure increase, pupils dilate, digestion ceases, and norepinephrine is secreted; the resistance stage where the stressors remain present and resistance remains above normal; and the exhaustion stage when bodily resources are depleted and physical and psychological breakdown are eminent.

        2. Selye's model focuses only on the physiological aspects of responding to stressors, not on how a person can respond cognitively or behaviorally.

    D. In the long run, the most effective way to deal with stress is to make relatively permanent changes in our behaviors as a result of the experience of stress.

        1. The stress we experience might be unpleasant, but it may produce positive consequences by forcing us to learn new options.

        2. Specific steps we can take to help alleviate the unpleasantness of stress in our lives include identifying the stressor, removing or negating the stressor, reappraising the situation, inoculating against future stressors, and taking time with important decisions.

        3. There are short-term actions we can take to combat the unpleasant feelings that accompany stress, such as learning techniques of relaxation, engaging in physical exercise, and seeking social support.

    E. Some reactions to stressors are maladaptive and ineffective, such as continuing to accept the same stress or behaving aggressively.

TOPIC 11B – Health Psychology

1. Explain health psychology and the assumptions made by psychologists working in the field.

2. Summarize the relationship between the Type A behavior pattern and coronary heart disease.

3. Discuss more current research contesting the role of the TABP in coronary heart disease.

4. Explain why psychologists care about smoking behaviors; describe the deleterious effects for smokers and nonsmokers.

5. Discuss some characteristics of people who successfully quit smoking.

6. Name and describe the characteristics of four sexually transmitted diseases that can be successfully treated.

7. Describe some characteristics of AIDS and its treatment that distinguish it from other STDs.

8. Explain the types of programs that have been designed to curb the transmission of AIDS, and discuss their effectiveness.

9. Discuss the psychological implications for persons with HIV and AIDS.

I.   Definition and Assumptions of Health Psychology

       A.   Health psychology became a division of the APA in 1978, and now has approximately 3,000 members.
       B.   Health psychology is the study of psychological or behavioral factors that affect physical health and illness.
       C.   The involvement of psychologists in the health field is based on four assumptions.
           1.   Certain behaviors increase the risk of certain chronic diseases.
           2.   Changes in behaviors can reduce the risk of certain diseases.
           3.   Changing behaviors is often easier and safer than treating many diseases.
           4.   Behavioral interventions are comparatively cost-effective.

II.   Psychological Factors That Influence Physical Health

       A.   In recognition of the role of psychologists in preventing disease and promoting good health, the Centers for Disease Control and the APA have initiated collaborative discussions.
       B.   There seems to be a positive correlation between some personality variables and physical health.
           1.   Type A behavior pattern, including competitive, impatient, and hostile behaviors, has been often associated with coronary heart disease.
           2.   Other research suggests anger and hostility, subcomponents of the Type A personality, may be responsible for coronary-prone risk.
           3.   Lynda Powell and her associates have found differences between Type A and Type B behavior patterns and risk in women.
       C.   More work needs to be done regarding the psychological factors that influence health.

III.   Promoting Health Behaviors

       A.   One role of health psychologists is to intervene to bring about changes in dangerous life-style behaviors.
           1.   Many of the leading causes of death in the U. S. are, in large part, behaviorally determined.
           2.   Interventions have been developed to change a wide range of behaviors.
       B.   Psychologists have been particularly active in helping people to stop smoking.
           1.   Smoking accounts for about 1/3 of all cancer deaths, yet it is the most preventable cause of death in America.
           2.   Analysis of 1985 data showed secondhand smoke killed 62,000 Americans and contributed to 200,000 nonfatal heart attacks.
           3.   Nearly 2.2 million adolescents between 12 and 17 smoke cigarettes, an estimated three thousand children begin smoking every day, and nine million children under the age of five years live with smokers.
           4.   Unfortunately, the success rate of programs to quit smoking have not been encouraging.
           5.   Psychologists have been reasonably successful in designing programs aimed at getting young people to refrain from smoking in the first place.
       C.   Sexually transmitted diseases–contagious diseases that are usually transmitted through sexual conduct–are an important focus of health psychology.
           1.   Sexually transmitted diseases affect millions every year, and for every one of these there may be two to five people who have a disease, but have not been diagnosed.
           2.   Attempts to prevent the transmission of these diseases involve psychological interventions to get people to change their behaviors.
           3.   Common sexually transmitted diseases have very unpleasant and serious symptoms and consequences.
           4.   Acquired immune deficiency syndrome (AIDS) is caused by a virus (HIV) that destroys the body's natural immune system.
           5.   Psychological interventions to decrease the incidence of AIDS have been multifaceted, involving education, the changing of attitudes, increasing motivation to engage in safe sexual practices, and providing people with negotiating skills.
           6.   Health officials are discouraged that, even with considerable knowledge about AIDS, few people seem willing to change their sexual practices.
           7.   Programs that go beyond just providing information and actively seek to change behaviors have been effective.

CHAPTER 12

THE PSYCHOLOGICAL DISORDERS

TOPIC 12A – Anxiety, Somatoform, Dissociative And Personality Disorders

Learning Objectives

1. Explain how psychological abnormality is defined.

2. Discuss some of the difficulties in defining abnormality.

3. Describe the DSM-IV, and discuss its advantages.

4. Discuss the advantages and disadvantages of a general classification scheme for mental disorders.

5. Explain "insanity."

6. Describe the symptoms of generalized anxiety disorder.

7. Explain "comorbidity" and its significance.

8. Define panic disorder.

9. Describe the essential characteristics of a phobic disorder.

10. Distinguish between obsessions and compulsions.

11. Describe the characteristics of obsessive-compulsive disorder.

12. Describe posttraumatic stress disorder.

13. Distinguish between hypochondriasis and conversion disorder.

14. Characterize the defining symptoms of the dissociative disorders.

15. Characterize personality disorders.

I. Just What Is "Abnormal"?

    A. Abnormal means maladaptive cognitions, affect, and/or behaviors that are at odds with social expectations and that result in distress and discomfort.

    B. The American Psychiatric Association publishes a classification for mental disorders called the Diagnostic and Statistical Manual of Mental Disorders (DSM) that has been revised several times.

        1. The latest version, the DSM-IV, is more than just an organized list of disorders in terms of symptoms.

        2. A single classification scheme provides a basis for communication about the disorder with other professionals.

    C. There are problems associated with any scheme of classifying disorders.

        1. Applying labels to people is often dehumanizing.

        2. It is easy to fall into the habit of believing that labels explain.

        3. Labels often create unfortunate and lasting stigmas, or negative attitudes, about people.

        4. Systems of classification tend to focus on the person and not the larger contexts in which individuals live.

        5. Comorbidity creates another problem for classification.

    D. Insanity is a legal term not a psychological term, and insanity generally requires that the person did not know or fully understand the consequences of her or his actions, could not discern differences between right and wrong, and was unable to exercise control over her or his actions.

    E. When discussing psychological disorders it's important to remember abnormal and normal are not two distinct categories, abnormal does not mean dangerous, abnormal does not mean bad, psychological disorders may occur in mild or moderate forms, and people will not be exactly alike.

II. Anxiety Disorders

    A. Anxiety is a general feeling of apprehension or dread accompanied by predictable physiological changes, and anxiety-based disorders are among the most common of all psychological disorders.

    B. Generalized anxiety disorder is characterized by persistent, chronic, and distressingly high levels of unattributable anxiety that doesn't seem to be brought on by anything specific in the person's environment.

    C. Panic disorder is characterized by acute anxiety attacks that are recurrent, unpredictable, and unprovoked.

        1. Between 1.5 and 3.5 percent of the population will experience panic disorder at some time in their lives, and it is often complicated by feelings of depression.

        2. Age of onset is between adolescence and the mid-twenties, and initial panic episodes are commonly associated with stress.

    D. Phobic disorders involve persistent, irrational fear that leads a person to avoid the feared object, activity, or situation and that is intense enough to be disruptive or debilitating.

        1. Specific phobias involve the physical environment, and social phobias are significant and persistent fears of social or performance situations.

        2. The prognosis for phobic disorders is good.

    E. Obsessive-compulsive disorder (OCD) is an anxiety disorder characterized by a pattern of recurrent obsessions (ideas or thoughts that involuntarily and persistently intrude into awareness) and compulsions (constantly intruding, repetitive acts or behaviors).

        1. Obsessive-compulsive disorder is much more common than once believed, affecting nearly 1 of every 200 teenagers, and as many as 5 million Americans total.

        2. Recent evidence suggests a biological basis for OCD.

        3. The prognosis for OCD is generally not very good.

    F. Posttraumatic stress disorder (PTSD) involves several symptoms that arise at some time well after experiencing a highly stressful event, such as reexperiencing the traumatic event, avoiding any possible reminders of the event, or increased arousal.

        1. Defining PTSD has made it possible to identify those who suffer from it, about two percent of the population according to current estimates.

        2. We often find comorbidity with PTSD, most commonly alcohol and substance abuse and depression.

        3. Some research suggests genetic factors may predispose persons to develop symptoms of PTSD.

III. Somatoform Disorders

    A. Somatoform disorders in some way involve physical, bodily symptoms or complaints for which there is no known physical cause.

    B. Hypochondriasis is the appropriate diagnosis for someone preoccupied with the fear of developing or having some serious disease.

    C. Conversion disorder, where the symptoms are not intentionally produced and cannot be explained by any physical disorder, is now rare, accounting for less than 5 percent of the anxiety-based disorders.

        1. In some cases, such as glove anesthesia, medical explanations run contrary to the symptoms.

        2. La belle indifference–an inappropriate lack of concern over one's condition–is a remarkable secondary symptom.

IV. Dissociative Disorders

    A. A person with a dissociative disorder seeks to escape from some aspect of life or personality that is seen as the source of stress, discomfort, or anxiety.

    B. Dissociative amnesia is a psychologically caused inability to recall important personal information, usually some traumatic incident.

    C. Dissociative fugue is a condition of amnesia accompanied by unexplained travel or change of location to escape stressful situations.

    D. Dissociative identity disorder is the existence within an individual of two or more distinct personalities, each of which is dominant at a particular time.

        1. Previously known as multiple personality disorder, there is often confusion between this disorder and schizophrenia.

        2. The change in personality is dramatic and extreme, implying a change in underlying consciousness, not just a change in behaviors.

        3. Individuals with dissociative identity disorder are unable to control or predict which personality will be dominant at any one time.

        4. Persons diagnosed with this disorder are often victims of child abuse, sexual abuse, or drug abuse, and are more likely to be women than men.

V. Personality Disorders

    A. Personality disorders are enduring patterns of perceiving, relating to, and thinking about the environment and one's self that are inflexible and maladaptive and that cause impaired functioning or distress.

    B. The DSM-IV lists several personality disorders.

        1. Paranoid personality disorder involves extreme unjustified sensitivity, suspiciousness, envy, and mistrust of others, coupled with a restricted range of emotional reactivity.

        2. Schizoid personality disorder is characterized by a lack of, and indifference to, interpersonal relationships.

        3. Persons with histrionic personality disorder are overly dramatic, reactive, and intensely expressive, and narcissistic personality disorder reflects a grandiose exaggeration of self-importance, a need for attention and admiration, and a tendency to set unrealistic goals.

        4. Avoidant personality disorder reflects an oversensitivity to potentially being rejected by others and an unwillingness to enter into relationships for fear of being rejected.

        5. People with dependent personality disorder demonstrate a poor self-image and lack of confidence; they allow and seek others to dominate and assume responsibility for their actions.

    C. Estimates of the prevalence of PDs are inexact because the disorders are difficult to diagnose accurately; the overall rate of PD is between 10 and 20 percent, but the rates of specific disorders are low.

    D. The prognosis is usually quite poor for personality disorders.

    E. There are several hypotheses attempting to explain the cause of personality disorders.

    F. Antisocial personality disorder refers to an exceptional lack of regard for the rights and property of others and performance of impulsive behaviors without regard for consequences.

        1. Fifteen to twenty percent of American prisoners have antisocial personality disorder.

        2. APD is more likely to be found among those of low SES status, those who live in urban settings, and those who have a history of antisocial behaviors beginning before age ten.

        3. APD is more often diagnosed in males; estimates put the disorder at about three percent of the population for males and one percent for females.

        4. APD is resistant to treatment, but some persons with APD experience spontaneous remission of symptoms in their early 40s.

TOPIC 12B – Alzheimer's Dementia, Mood Disorders, And Schizophrenia

Learning Objectives

1. Describe the characteristics of Alzheimer's disease.

2. Discuss the potential causes of Alzheimer's disease.

3. Explain the different mood disorders.

4. Discuss the prevalence and the potential causes of mood disorders.

5. Explain potential reasons for the gender differential in mood disorders.

6. Distinguish between the positive and negative symptoms of schizophrenia.

7. Discuss the factors suspected as causes of schizophrenia.

I. Alzheimer's Dementia

    A. Dementia is a marked loss of intellectual abilities in which memory is poor and deteriorates, and judgment is adversely affected.

    B. A slow deterioration of one's intellectual functioning is the most common symptom associated with Alzheimer's disease, beginning with problems of recent memory and mild personality changes.

    C. First thought to be an inevitable consequence of aging, Alzheimer's is no longer referred to this way.

    D. Approximately four million Americans are afflicted with Alzheimer's disease, and over 11,000 patients die each year.

    E. Although the major symptoms of Alzheimer's disease are psychological, four major symptoms characterize brain tissue in such patients.

        1. A mass of tangled protein fibers is evident.

        2. Plaques, waste material, degenerated nerve fibers that wrap around a core of protein, are present.

        3. Several small cavities in the brain fill with fluid and debris, and some structures of the brain atrophy.

        4. Unfortunately, these signs can be found in normal brains, and their causes are unknown.

    F. The cause of Alzheimer's is still unknown, although there is probably a genetic basis; the role of a particular protein molecule that forms plagues in Alzheimer's brains is also under investigation, and other possibilities include a decrease in acetylcholine, or perhaps low levels of toxins.

II. Mood Disorders

    A. Mood disorders (affective disorders) clearly demonstrate some disturbance in one's emotional reactions or feelings, and are differentiated by the extremeness and intensity of mood.

        1. Major depression, diagnosed two times more in women than in men, is a mood disorder characterized by inexplicable moods of sadness and hopelessness, accompanied by a loss of pleasure or interest in usual activities.

        2. Dysthymia is a mild case of major depression that is inexplicable and chronic, with recurrent pessimism, low energy level, and low self-esteem.

        3. Bipolar disorder is a mood disorder that affects nearly two million Americans, and is characterized by depression with intermittent periods of mania–a heightened euphoria and increased activity.

    B. Depression is caused by a number of different, but potentially interrelated, causes.

        1. Although there is evidence of a genetic predisposition for bipolar mood disorder, evidence for a genetic basis for depression is not as strong.

        2. Attention has been focused on neurotransmitters that appear to influence mood directly (biogenic amines), and recent studies of the brains of people with mood disorders have found some of the same structural abnormalities associated with schizophrenia.

        3. Learning theorists have attributed depression to experience, but the direction of causality is indeterminate; other theorists argue that the causes of depression are mainly cognitive.

III. Schizophrenia

    A. Schizophrenia is a diagnosis given to a number of specified disorders that share a distortion of reality and a retreat from others, accompanied by disturbances in perception, thinking, affect, and behavior.

    B. Schizophrenia occurs around the world at the same rate (about one percent of the population), and displays negative symptoms such as emotional and social withdrawal, reduced energy and motivation, apathy, and poor attention; positive symptoms such as hallucinations and delusions; and positive disorganized symptoms including disorders of thinking and speech, bizarre behaviors, and inappropriate affect.

    C. The causes of schizophrenia are tentative and multidimensional.

        1. The risk of being diagnosed as a schizophrenic increases if there is a family history of the disorder.

        2. Several lines of research involving dopamine have highlighted the role of the brain and biochemical processes in schizophrenia.

        3. Schizophrenics may have unusually large ventricles, and a lack of balance between the two hemispheres; there may also be a loss of tissue in and around the limbic system, larger crevices in the surface of the cortex, and a smaller thalamus.

        4. Current general consensus does not support the position that schizophrenia develops in response to early experiences within the family unit.

CHAPTER 13

TREATMENT AND THERAPY

TOPIC 13A – History and Biomedical Treatments

Learning Objectives

1. Trace the history of the treatment of people with psychological disorders

2. Discuss later "enlightened" treatment and the people involved in the movement.

3. Define lobotomy, and discuss its use both past and present.

4. Describe ECT and its current use.

5. Discuss treatment with antipsychotic drugs, listing the various drugs and their effects.

6. Discuss treatment with antidepressant drugs, including the effect of the drugs and their side effects.

7. Discuss treatment with antianxiety drugs and the dangers of their use.

8. Explain the reasons for, and the problems involved with, deinstitutionalization.

I. A Historical Perspective

    A. How people have been treated for psychological disorders has been consistent with the prevailing view of what caused the disorder.
        1. Greeks and Romans believed that mentally disturbed individuals had offended the gods; Hippocrates believed mental disorders had physical causes, and he tried to demystify psychological disorders.
        2. During the Middle Ages (1000 to 1500 A.D.) the mentally ill were seen as possessed by, or under the spell of, the devil or evil spirits, and treatment consisted primarily of torture.
        3. In the eighteenth and nineteenth centuries a few enlightened individuals, including Philippe Pinel, Benjamin Rush, Dorothea Dix, and Clifford Beers, worked against a backdrop of misery and despair.
    B. Conditions have improved greatly during the past fifty years, but there is a long way to go in fighting prejudice against persons with psychological disorders.

II. Biomedical Treatments of Psychological Disorders

    A. Treatments that are medical in nature are not used by psychologists, but psychologists make recommendations and refer clients for such treatment.
    B. Psychosurgery refers to surgical procedures designed to affect psychological or behavioral reactions.
        1. Severing of the corpus callosum has been used to alleviate the symptoms of extreme epilepsy.
        2. Small lesions in the limbic system have reduced or eliminated violent behaviors.
        3. Surgical techniques are being used to treat some cases of Parkinson's disease.
        4. A prefrontal lobotomy severs the major neural connections between the prefrontal lobes of the cerebral cortex and the lower brain centers.
    C. Electroconvulsive therapy (ECT), introduced in 1937, involves passing an electric current (70 to 150 volts) across a tranquilized patient's head for a fraction of a second.
        1. ECT is most effective for patients suffering depression accompanied by other symptoms such as hallucinations or delusions.
        2. No more than twelve treatments should be given, and these should be spread over a long period of time, but after only ten to twelve treatments, many patients remain free of symptoms for months.
        3. About 110,000 patients still receive ECT yearly, although drug therapy has reduced the need to use ECT.
    D. One of the most significant scientific achievements of the last half of the twentieth century has been psychoactive drugs, chemicals that have their effect on a person's affect, behavior, or cognitions.
        1. Antipsychotic drugs, primarily designed to treat schizophrenia, reduce the severity of, and occasionally may even eliminate, psychotic symptoms, and mostly work by blocking receptor sites for the neurotransmitter, dopamine.
        2. Antidepressant drugs–including Prozac, Effexor, and Lithium–elevate mood, and can be used with panic disorder and generalized anxiety disorder as well as depression, but most antidepressants produce unfortunate side effects such as intellectual confusion, increased perspiration, and weight gain.
        3. Antianxiety drugs (or tranquilizers) help reduce the felt aspect of anxiety, and some are muscle relaxers, but the tranquilizing effects of the drugs are not long-lasting, and dependency and addiction can develop from which withdrawal is difficult.

III. Deinstitutionalization: Blessing or Curse?

    A. Within the past forty years, the shift in mental health care has been to deinstitutionalization, the releasing of mental patients to return to family and community.
    B. Reasons for deinstitutionalization included a concern for the rights of the patients, often overcrowded and inhumane conditions, the availability of drug therapy, and the anticipated availability of community mental health centers.
    C. The benefits of deinstitutionalization have been questioned because resources are often minimal, many patients require assistance from the welfare system, housing is often unavailable, community mental health centers are fruitless if patients do not seek their support, and many released patients stop taking their medication, leading to recurrence of symptoms.

TOPIC 13B – The Psychotherapies

1. List and describe the different types of mental health professionals.

2. Describe Freudian psychoanalysis, and define its major features and techniques.

3. Explain how psychoanalysis is different today from the way it was practiced by Freud.

4. Contrast the essential characteristics of client-centered therapy with those of gestalt therapy.

5. Name and describe the techniques used in behavior therapy.

6. Describe rational-emotive therapy and cognitive restructuring therapy.

7. Discuss the advantages of group therapy.

8. List the two assumptions underlying family therapy.

9. Discuss the effectiveness of psychotherapy in general and whether any one type is more effective than others.

I.   Who Provides Psychotherapy?

A. Thirty years ago only 13 percent of the population sought psychotherapy at any time during their lives, now the number is more like 30 percent.
B. Mental health professionals, usually from middle-class backgrounds, often specialize (e.g., work with children, particular cultures, etc.).
C. Clinical psychologists usually have a Ph.D. in psychology, have spent a year in internship, and have extensive training in psychological testing.
D. Psychiatrists serve an internship and a residency at a mental hospital, and they are the only therapists who can use biomedical treatments.
E. Counseling psychologists usually have a Ph.D. in psychology, but focus on less severe psychological problems.
F. A licensed professional counselor has a degree in counselor education, has met state requirements for a license to perform psychotherapy, and generally is found in schools and family counseling and drug abuse programs.
G. Psychoanalyst is a special label given either to a clinical psychologist or a psychiatrist who has also received intensive training in the methods of Freudian psychoanalysis.
H. Clinical social workers can and do engage in a variety of psychotherapies, but their traditional role has been involvement in family and group therapy.
I. Psychotherapy may be offered by a number of other professionals and paraprofessionals, but certification laws prohibit them from advertising themselves as psychologists.

II.   Psychoanalytic Techniques

A. Psychoanalysis began with Sigmund Freud, and is based on a number of assumptions, most of them having to do with the nature of conflict and the unconscious mind.
    1. Freud believed life is often a struggle to resolve conflicts between naturally opposing forces, and this struggle produces anxiety.
    2. To get rid of anxiety it is necessary to enter the unconscious mind, identify the conflict, bring it out into the open, and resolve it.
B. The main task of the therapist is to interpret what is being expressed by the patient and to be always on the lookout for repressed conflict.
C. Procedures and processes used in Freudian psychoanalysis to search for repressed conflicts include free association, analyzing resistance, and analyzing a patient's dreams.
D. In recent years, psychoanalysis has become much less common, and strict, Freudian psychoanalysis has become quite rare.

III. Humanistic Techniques

A. All humanistic approaches are concerned with self-examination, personal growth, and development; therapy is devised to assist with those processes.
B. Client-centered, or Rogerian, therapy is probably the therapy that best typifies the humanistic approach.
    1. The focus is on the present, and on one's feelings or affect, not one's cognitions.
    2. The therapist is an active, empathic listener, and attempts to reflect, rather than interpret, how the client is feeling.
    3. The therapist expresses unconditional positive regard toward the patient.
C. Gestalt therapy is associated with Fritz Perls, and shares many of the same goals as client-centered therapy, but differs from client-centered therapy in that the therapist is more actively involved and challenges the client.

IV.   Behavioral Techniques

A. Rather than a single unified approach, behavior therapy is a collection of many specific techniques based on principles of learning.
B. Systematic desensitization is the application of classical conditioning procedures to alleviate extreme feelings of anxiety: the subject is first instructed in methods of relaxation, then an anxiety hierarchy is constructed, after which the subject relaxes and focuses on each item in the hierarchy sequentially.

C. Exposure and response prevention, where patients are exposed to whatever evokes their obsessional thinking but are not allowed to engage in their usually compulsive behavior, is a form of behavior therapy that has shown promise as treatment for obsessive-compulsive disorder.

D. In aversion therapy, a stimulus that produces a pleasant response is paired with an aversive, painful, unpleasant stimulus until the pleasant stimulus becomes unpleasant.

E. In contingency management and contingency contracting appropriate behaviors lead to rewards and opportunities to do valued things, and inappropriate behaviors lead to aversive stimulation and fewer opportunities.
1. It is called contingency management when the therapist controls rewards and punishments.
2. Contingency contracting amounts to establishing a contract with a client so that certain behaviors will result in certain rewards, which often involves establishing a token economy.
3. This technique is particularly effective in institutions and with young children.

F. Modeling involves the acquisition of a new, appropriate response through the imitation of a model.
1. Some phobias, especially in children, can be overcome through modeling.
2. Assertiveness training involves many processes and often relies on modeling.

V. Cognitive Techniques

A. The principle behind cognitive therapy is that to change how one feels and acts, therapy should first be directed at changing how one thinks.

B. Rational-emotive therapy (RET), associated with Albert Ellis, has as its basic premise the belief that psychological problems arise when a person tries to interpret what happens on the basis of irrational beliefs.
1. Ellis believes the irrational beliefs that people should always be loved for everything they do and that it's better to avoid problems than to face them are very common.
2. Rather than waiting for self discovery, a rational-emotive therapist would point out irrational beliefs and suggest changes.

C. Cognitive restructuring therapy is similar to RET, but is much less confrontational and direct.
1. A therapist offers the patient opportunities to test or demonstrate his or her beliefs.
2. Cognitive restructuring therapy has proven very successful in the treatment of depression.

VI. Group Approaches

A. Group therapy is a general label applied to a variety of situations in which a number of people are involved in a therapeutic setting at the same time.
1. In standard group therapy, a number of clients are brought together at one time (with a therapist's guidance) to share their feelings and experiences.
2. With group approaches clients become aware they're not the only ones with problems, they have a sense of support from other group members, and they may learn new and more effective ways of interacting with others.

B. Family therapy is a variety of group therapy that focuses on the roles, interdependence, and communication skills of family members.
1. Getting the family involved in therapy benefits patients with a wide range of disorders.
2. Underlying this approach are the assumptions that each individual family member is a part of, and impacts, a family system and that difficulties within families stem from improper methods of communication.

VII. Evaluating Psychotherapy

A. Evaluating psychotherapy has proven to be a very difficult task.

B. Psychotherapy is effective compared to doing nothing.
1. More treatment is better than less treatment, and research shows that the sooner one begins therapy, the better the prognosis.
2. In some cases, time-limited therapy works as well as unlimited sessions, and some therapists are simply more effective than others.

C. There is little data on how people respond without therapy, we can't agree on what we mean by recovery, and there is often concern about how to measure or assess outcomes; nevertheless, recent meta-analyses have shown positive results for psychotherapy.

D. When comparing psychotherapy methods, in general, there are no differences, although some types are better for specific problems.

CHAPTER 14

SOCIAL PSYCHOLOGY

TOPIC 14A – Social Cognitions: Attitudes, Attributions, and Attractions

Learning Objectives

1. Define attitude and list and explain the three components of an attitude.

2. Explain how attitudes are acquired.

3. Define cognitive dissonance, and explain how it relates to attitude change.

4. Describe the two routes that may be used to process persuasive information and how they explain attitude change.

5. Explain two characteristics of a communicator that may affect persuasion, describing how the characteristics relate to the route used in processing the persuasive message.

6. List the two basic types of attributions and the three types of information used in making attributions.

7. List four specific attributional biases, explaining how attributions become distorted or biased.

8. Describe the four theoretical models of interpersonal attraction.

9. Know the four determinants of interpersonal attraction and their effects.

I. Preview

    A. Social psychology is the field of psychology that is concerned with how people influence the thoughts, feelings, and behaviors of one another and that relies on experimentation and other scientific methods as sources of knowledge.

    B. Social cognition involves questions about what social world information we store in our memories and about how that information influences social judgments, choices, attractions, and behaviors.

II. Attitudes

    A. An attitude is a relatively stable disposition to evaluate some object or event.

    B. The affective component of attitudes consists of our feelings about the attitudinal object, the behavioral component consists of our response or action tendencies toward the object of our attitude, and the cognitive component includes our beliefs or thoughts about the attitudinal object.

    C. Attitude formation appears to occur through learning.

        1. Some attitudes are acquired through the simple associative process of classical conditioning or as a result of the direct reinforcement of behaviors consistent with an attitudinal position (operant conditioning).

        2. When we observe others gaining reinforcers for having and expressing some attitude, we are likely to adopt that attitude ourselves (observational learning).

    D. Conscious, planned attempts to change someone's attitude are called persuasion.

        1. Cognitive dissonance theory proposes that attitudes get changed when people attempt to realign inconsistent attitudes and behaviors.

        2. There may be two different pathways, or routes, involved in changing someone's attitudes: a central route involving the nature and quality of the message, and a peripheral route involving issues beyond the content of the message itself.

III. Attribution Theory

    A. Attribution theory has to do with understanding the cognitions we use in trying to explain behavior, both our own and that of others.

    B. Internal (dispositional) attributions explain the source of behavior in terms of some characteristic of the person, and external (situational) attributions explain the sources of behavior in terms of the situation or social context outside the individual.

    C. When making attributional judgments, people tend to rely on information concerning the distinctiveness, consensus, and consistency of the targeted behavior.

    D. The trait inference process tends to draw an inference about the presence of some trait that led to a targeted behavior and revise or modify that attribution as a function of the situation, but the situational inference process works in the reverse direction.

    E. We tend to make various errors in our social thinking, including the fundamental attribution error, the just-world hypothesis, the self-serving bias, and the actor-observer bias.

IV. Interpersonal Attraction

    A. Interpersonal attraction reflects the extent to which a person has formed positive feelings and beliefs about another person and is prepared to act on those affects and cognitions.

    B. Social psychologists have put forth a number of theoretical models to explain the bases of interpersonal attraction.

        1. The reinforcement model claims that we tend to be attracted to people we associate with rewarding experiences.

        2. The social exchange model emphasizes comparison of the costs and benefits associated with a relationship, and the equity model–an extension of the social-exchange theory–states that all members of a relationship want to feel they are getting a fair deal.

        3. Attachment theory suggests interpersonal relationships can be classified as secure, avoidant, or anxious/ambivalent–depending on the attitudes that one has about such relationships.

    C. The four most common factors affecting interpersonal attraction are reciprocity, proximity, physical attractiveness, and similarity.

TOPIC 14B – Social Influence

Learning Objectives

1. Discuss the methodology and findings of Asch's studies.

2. Discuss Milgram's studies of obedience.

3. Explain how the presence of others affects helping behavior.

4. Describe Latané and Darley's cognitive model of helping.

5. Discuss the psychological processes that account for what is called the social inhibition of helping.

6. Explain social loafing and discuss some factors that affect the process.

7   Explain social facilitation and discuss some factors that affect the process.

8. Describe group polarization.

9. Discuss groupthink.

10. List conditions under which groups make better decisions than individuals.

I. Conformity

A. We modify our behavior so that it is consistent with the behavior of others, a process called conformity.
B. The Asch studies showed that conformity occurred 37 percent of the time, and 75 percent of Asch's subjects conformed to group pressure at least once.

II. Obedience to Authority

A. Milgram's obedience studies reported the astonishing finding that 65 percent of subjects obeyed the experimenter's demands and (ostensibly) shocked another subject all the way to the highest shock value.
B. Factors shown to reduce the level of shock the subjects would administer included putting the learner and the teacher in the same room, having the experimenter deliver his orders over the phone, and having two disobedient confederates accompany the subject.
C. The ethics of Milgram's experiment were questioned, but Milgram reported he took great care to debrief his subjects after each session; nevertheless, Milgram's studies were responsible for enhanced ethical guidelines for psychological research.

III. Bystander Intervention

A. Latané and Darley developed a model of bystander intervention that incorporates situational factors and suggests a series of cognitive events that must occur before a bystander will intervene, including noticing something is happening, interpreting it as an emergency, deciding that she or he is responsible, and deciding how to implement the helping behavior.
B. Psychological processes that may account for the bystander effect include audience inhibition, pluralistic ignorance, and diffusion of responsibility.
C. Research leads to the conclusion that help is more likely with an individual than with a group; the bystander effect is a robust phenomenon.

IV. Social Loafing and Facilitation

A. Social loafing is the tendency to work less as the size of the group in which one is working becomes larger.
    1. Social loafing is considerably less likely in collectivist cultures that place a high value on participation in group activities.
    2. Even in individualistic cultures, social loafing can be reduced if group members believe their efforts are special and required for group success and/or that their efforts can be identified or evaluated.
B. Social facilitation means that performance improves due to the presence of others; social interference refers to impaired performance due to the presence of others.
C. Zajonc noticed that social facilitation occurred whenever the behavior under study was simple, routine, or very well-learned; if the dominant response is correct, the behavior is facilitated–if incorrect, social interference occurs.

V. Decision Making in Groups

A. Many decisions we face are the sort that must be made in groups.
B. Although there is logic in the belief that group problem-solving should be superior to the efforts of individuals, group polarization refers to a tendency for groups to move to more extreme positions.
    1. Open discussion gives group members an opportunity to hear persuasive arguments they have not previously considered, which leads to a strengthening of their original attitudes.
    2. After comparing positions with other group members, some members feel pressure to catch up to those with more extreme positions.
C. Groupthink refers to an excessive concern for reaching a consensus, particularly in cohesive groups, to the extent that critical evaluations are withheld; it may be reflected in several key historical events, including the Bay of Pigs invasion and the escalation of the Vietnam War.
D. Situations exist in which groups are more efficient decision makers than individuals working alone.
    1. Groups are useful when problems are complex and require skills and abilities beyond those possessed by one person.
    2. Group decision making can identify errors individuals may miss.

CHAPTER 15

INDUSTRIAL/ORGANIZATIONAL, ENVIRONMENTAL, AND SPORTS PSYCHOLOGY

TOPIC 15A – Industrial/Organizational Psychology

Learning Objectives

1. Explain what is involved in doing a job analysis.

2. Describe some of the information sources that can be used in making personnel decisions.

3. List some of the factors that need to be considered in the design, implementation, and evaluation of a training program.

4. Summarize the factors that affect the motivation of workers to do a good job.

5. Define job satisfaction and the quality of work life.

6. Describe the relationship between job satisfaction and job productivity.

7. Discuss two approaches that can be taken to improve worker safety.

I. Preview

   A. Industrial/organizational psychology specializes in the study of affect, behavior, and cognitions in work settings, and is one of the fastest growing areas of specialization in psychology.
   B. I/O psychologists are concerned with how best to fit the right person to a given job, and they also study how best to fit a job to the person.

II. Fitting the Person to the Job

   A. The main issues involved in fitting the right person to the job from the I/O psychologist's perspective are personnel selection, training, and motivation.
   B. A job analysis is a process that results in a complete and specific description of a job.
   C. Picking people who can do good work requires a variety of techniques and sources of information, including a well-constructed job application and a structured employment interview, which tend to be much more valid than unstructured interviews.
   D. Personnel selection often involves the administration and interpretation of psychological tests.
      1. Situational tests are those in which applicants role-play some of the tasks they may be hired to do.
      2. The validity of a test is crucial; it should measure a construct related to performance.
      3. An assessment center approach involves an intensive period of evaluation where several applicants are brought together with company executives and a team of psychologists and given a battery of tests and interviews, perhaps including situational tests such as the in-basket technique.
   E. Training or retraining, one of the major–and most costly–concerns of business, industry, and government, will become even more critical as the number of people entering the work force decreases.
      1. Increased sensitivity and communication training for dealing with employees from a variety of ethnic and cultural backgrounds is becoming more common.
      2. To develop a successful training program, an assessment of instructional needs is completed; after that, specific training techniques must be developed, and it's important to use a variety of techniques for different needs and objectives.
      3. Training effectiveness must be evaluated.
   F. I/O psychologists have long been interested in how to motivate employees to do good work.
      1. Work motivation refers to three interrelated processes: arousing the worker to do a task, directing the worker to do a particular task, and sustaining the work at the task.
      2. Expectancy theory (Vroom) takes the view that workers make logical choices based on their beliefs, judgments, and expectations about rewards contingent on levels of performance.
      3. Equity theory takes the view that workers are motivated to match their inputs and outcomes with those of fellow workers in similar positions.
      4. Goal setting, which is currently receiving much research interest, assumes that workers are best motivated to perform a task for which the goals are clearly and specifically detailed.

III. Fitting the Job to the Person

   A. Job satisfaction is an attitude or a collection of feelings about one's job or job experiences.
   B. Younger workers tend to be more dissatisfied, and satisfaction is positively related to the perceived level or status of one's job or occupation, but there are some cultural and ethnic differences in job satisfaction.
   C. Managers and executives often assume a causal relationship between satisfaction and productivity, but research suggests the relationship is complex and weak at best.
   D. In 1993 there were 6,271 job-related deaths, up from 6,217 in 1992; accidents in the workplace cost the United States over $100 billion a year in lost wages, insurance, medical expenses, and property loss.
      1. The Occupational Safety and Health Administration (OSHA) is the federal agency in charge of job safety, unfortunately, they often don't get to inspect and intervene in potentially dangerous situations.
      2. So far, personality traits reliably related to accidents have not been identified; nevertheless, the less qualified, less well-trained, or less motivated a worker is for a job, the more likely the person will have an accident, and workers younger than 25 or older than 55 have more accidents.
      3. The engineering approach attempts to reduce accidents through the design and implementation of safe equipment and procedures, and it has been the most successful.

74

TOPIC 15B – Environmental and Sports Psychology

Learning Objectives

1. Define environmental psychology, and list some of the issues that environmental psychologists study.

2. Define the concepts of personal space and territoriality.

3. Distinguish between population density and crowding.

4. List the positive and negative aspects of city living.

5. Describe the effects of noise, extreme temperature, and neurotoxins on behavior.

6. Explain how applied behavior analysis programs can have a positive impact on the environment.

7. Discuss some of the ways psychologists become involved in sports and athletics.

8. Explain the ways mental imagery helps athletes to obtain peak performance.

I. Psychology and the Environment

    A. Environmental psychology is the field of applied psychology that studies the effect of the general environment on organisms within it, and conversely, how the organisms affect their environments.

    B. The study of the effects of invading personal space and territory has been an active research area for environmental psychologists.
        1. Personal space is the imaginary, mobile "bubble" of space surrounding people that is reserved for intimate relationships, the extent of which depends on the situation as well as on several other factors, including age, gender, cultural background, and who the intruder is.
        2. Territoriality is the setting off and marking of a piece of territory (a location) as one's own: primary territories are defined as ours alone and no one else's; secondary territories, more flexible and less well defined, are not used for expressing personal identity; and public territories are those we tend to occupy for only a short time.

    C. Concern about city living, overcrowding, and the consequences of urbanization has been a part of environmental psychology for over thirty years.
        1. Combined, the world's biggest cities are growing at a rate of one million persons a week, and these large cities will be home to more than half the world's population soon after the turn of the twenty-first century.
        2. Prompted by research on crowding with rats, early investigations found correlations between population density and negative behavioral consequences, but it later became clear that translation of the data from rats to humans was not straightforward.
        3. Population density is an objective, quantitative measure of the number of persons per unit of area; crowding, a psychological concept, is the subjective feeling of discomfort caused by a perceived lack of space, and is a negative condition that tends to produce negative consequences.
        4. The challenge of environmental psychologists is to help urban planners and architects design living spaces in areas of high density that minimize the subjective experience of crowding.

    D. Noise, temperature, and environmental toxins can have a profound effect on behavior.
        1. Noise is any intrusive, unwanted, or excessive experience of sound, and becomes most stressful when it is loud, high-pitched, and unpredictable.
        2. As temperatures increase, performance may deteriorate and violent crimes increase.
        3. Environmental psychologists are concerned with toxins in the environment and their poisonous effects on the nervous system.

    E. Psychologists active in establishing environmentally beneficial programs aimed at changing behaviors, such as applied behavior analysis, have found positive effects for such programs when consequences are tied to a person's response, and not to some potentially long-term outcome.

II. Psychology and Sport

    A. Sport psychology is the application of psychological principles to sport and physical activity at all levels of skill development.

    B. Research analyzing the psychological characteristics of athletes has been less than satisfactory and tends to confirm the obvious: athletes tend to score higher than nonathletes on tests of assertion, dominance, aggression, and need for achievement and lower on such traits as anxiety, depression, and fatigue than nonathletes.

    C. Psychologists help athletes to be sensitive to maintaining high levels of arousal while keeping appropriate levels of concentration on the task so as to maximize performance.
        1. The athlete in competition needs to be fully aroused and motivated to perform.
        2. The concept of a "hot hand" refers to a string or cluster of successful performances greater than chance would predict, but there is little evidence for a "hot hand" in sports.
        3. In a similar vein, sport psychologists claim the idea of a home field advantage is exaggerated, particularly in important games.
        4. Mental practice, or "imagery," combined with physical practice has proven quite beneficial in attaining peak athletic performance.